September 25, 1999 dinner on SS *Jeremiah O'Brien*

Based on the coastwise steamer *Yale*
of the Los Angeles Steamship Company
B.V. White, U.S.N.R. Commander
July 23, 1935

APPETIZERS
Victoria Canape
Assorted Olives

SOUP
Minestrone

FISH
Baked Chinook Salmon with
Anchovy Sauce

ENTREE
Roast Prime Ribs of Beef, *au Jus*

VEGETABLE
Garlic Mashed Potatoes
Saute of Italian Squash

BREAD
Dinner Rolls

DESSERTS
Green Apple Pie
Steamed Ginger Pudding with
Whiskey Sauce

BEVERAGES
Coffee

To Raylene:

Thank you for coming
with me today. All the best
to you.

Walt Wright
10/7/01
San Francisco

RECIPES FROM A COAL-FIRED STOVE*

THE
SS *JEREMIAH O'BRIEN*
COOKBOOK

by

Capt. Walter W. Jaffee

*adjusted for gas and electric stoves

THE GLENCANNON PRESS

MARITIME BOOKS

PALO ALTO
2001

Art Director: S.L. Hecht

Copyright © 2001 by Walter W. Jaffee
Published by The Glencannon Press
P.O. Box 341, Palo Alto, CA 94302
Tel. 800-711-8985
www.glencannon.com

First Edition, first printing.

**Library of Congress Cataloging-in-Publication Data
available from publisher on request.**

DEDICATION

To
Bev and Wes Masterson,
who have served every meal

ACKNOWLEDGMENTS

This book would not exist but for the spirit of volunteerism found on the *Jeremiah O'Brien*. The crew and the ship together embody a rare spirit of cooperation and enthusiasm that is contagious. From the most mundane tasks — chipping paint, wiping engines — to the biggest challenges — replacing a main engine bearing, installing a sanitation system — they pull together, work hard and can always be depended upon. This cooperative, can-do spirit is especially visible in the galley which, with its giant coal-fired stove, can be a hot, crowded place. Yet, the attitude is always, "how do we make it work" and "what can I do to help."

A museum ship is always creatively searching for funds. One of the most popular and successful efforts are the raffles conducted during the ship's annual cruises. Passengers buy chances for prizes, one of which is a special dinner for eight cooked aboard the ship. The dinners are based on historic ship menus. I'm part of the crew that cooks these raffle prize dinners. This book is in response to all those who asked for some of the shipboard recipes that the dinner crew, and the *Jeremiah O'Brien*'s regular galley crew use.

First off, I'd like to thank the chief steward, Jim Hallstrom, for allowing me access to the galley equipment and range. It is his domain, which he runs with watchful care. Capt. Ed Lodigiani, Rich Vannucci and Joe Guzzetta have been a great help in teaching me some of the tricks of cooking on the ship's formidable stove. Rich and Joe were also kind enough to provide recipes for some of the crew favorites that are included in this book.

My "partner in crime" in these cooking endeavors is Aldred Chipman. I couldn't do it without his capable hands, good ideas, careful attention to detail and wry sense of humor. He also provides the beer (usually, appropriately, Liberty Ale) on those long, hot days when we're chopping, mixing and cooking for that evening's raffle prize dinner.

Bev and Wes Masterson, to whom this book is dedicated, are in a league by themselves. Bev manages the ship's store. After a long day in No. 3 hold, she comes up to do a magnificent job of setting the tables and adding the extra touches that transform this plain room into an elegant dining parlor. She makes the officers' saloon look regal. She and Wes also act as our waiters for these dinners, presenting calm, smiling faces to our guests when all may be chaos in the galley. Their help is truly priceless.

There have been many others who helped at various times: Darcy Chipman, Barry Hensley, Diana Jaffee, Jason Jaffee, Clyde Matsumoto, Pat Matsumoto, Joe Milcic, John Rivers and Irene Williams. If I'm forgetting anyone, I apologize and thank you as well.

Finally, I'd like to thank my publisher for her patience, her skill and her good judgement in keeping me focused on the work at hand.

Contents

INTRODUCTION

Cooking is a great way to relax. Start with a recipe, add a dash of imagination, a pinch of creativity and soon your cares vanish as you lose yourself in a world of magic. In fact, a cook is like an alchemist, who, in medieval times, was believed to have the power to transform lead into gold. A good cook can take the most ordinary bunch of raw ingredients, combine them and create something golden that appeals to all of a diner's senses.

I got interested in shipboard cooking because of a breakfast dish called a "steam schooner." Steam schooners were small ships that plied the Pacific Coast from just after the Gold Rush in the 1850s until the Second World War. They were put out of business by economics. Highways and trucks made it cheaper to transport goods up and down the coast by road than by sea.

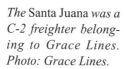

The Santa Juana *was a C-2 freighter belonging to Grace Lines. Photo: Grace Lines.*

The steam schooners were operated by hard-working, heavy-eating sailors, many of Scandinavian descent. One of their favorite breakfast meals was a stack of pancakes topped with at least two fried eggs. Because they liked it so much and they worked on steam schooners, the dish became known by that intriguing name.

My first acquaintance with the "steam schooner" was on my first ship as a cadet out of the U.S. Merchant Marine Academy at Kings Point, New York. She was the *Santa Juana* and she ran from the United States west coast to the west coast of South America. The officers and crew lived mostly in the Pacific Northwest and came to Grace Lines (the operator of the ship) through some of the older shipping companies with ties to the steam schooner lines — Alaska Steamship Company, Pope and Talbot and Grace Line. The meals on the *Santa Juana* were partly dictated by their background and "steam schooners" were frequently on the menu.

Another dish we had at breakfast was "tongues and sounds." This was the tongue and surrounding mouth area of a salmon which was preserved in salt brine. It was soaked in fresh water overnight to

This officers' mess on a tanker is similar to ours on the Santa Juana. *Photo: Standard Oil Co. (N.J.)*

remove the salt, then fried or boiled for breakfast. I never liked the dish but I liked knowing what it was. The same goes for salmon bellies. Considered a delicacy by some of the crew, they made a strong, salty counterpoint to one's morning eggs and toast.

A few years ago I noticed that when the conversation turned to cooking and meals aboard ship, fewer and fewer people knew what a "steam schooner" was. That's what got me interested in shipboard cooking. It was a way to keep those old dishes alive. And that's what got me interested in writing this cookbook. It, too, is a way to keep some of the old dishes alive; to record them before they're lost.

Walter W. Jaffee
Menlo Park
April 2001

A coal-fired stove has its own character and personality. It can be temperamental and comforting at the same time. Photo: author.

PREFACE

There's something very comforting about the warm, orange-red glow of a coal fire. The color is cheery, the heat is soothing and the odor is distinct. It brings back memories of campfires under starry skies, evening barbecues, and perhaps touches an ancestral chord we share across thousands of years — the family gathering for the evening meal. It is satisfying, a balm to the soul.

Such a fire can be found in the galley range of the SS *Jeremiah O'Brien*. Launched in 1943 at New England Shipbuilding's South Portland Shipyard in Portland, Maine, the *O'Brien* was one of those Liberty ships built in World War II and seen for decades afterward on the world's oceans. The Liberty design came from a British tramp out of the previous century; a ship whose engines and galley were fueled with coal.

Adapting the design to American World War II standards included changing the engines from coal to oil. But in the earlier ships, such as the *O'Brien*, the coal-

The Jeremiah O'Brien *at San Francisco's Pier 45 with the Golden Gate Bridge in the background. Photo: Marvin Jensen.*

fired stove was retained because it was simple to manufacture in the large quantities needed at the time.

For me, cooking is a hobby, something that's relaxing and enjoyable. With a gas or electric stove, you follow the recipe directions, set the controls to the correct heat and take the food off or out, as the case may be, at the proper time. But I quickly learned that is not the case on the *O'Brien*'s coal-fired stove. Here was a challenge!

The only temperature control on the *O'Brien*'s galley range is the amount of coal you put in the firebox, the damper adjustment, and where on the stove or in the oven you place what you're cooking. The top of the stove is one smooth expanse of metal. You slide your pots around — nearer or farther from the firebox. There are two ovens — one next to the firebox, the other farther away.

Just a few of the ingredients that go into a raffle prize "dinner for eight." Photo: S. Rose.

And it gets more complicated. Some types of coal burn faster and hotter than others. Larger pieces burn hotter than smaller pieces. And you have to plan ahead. It takes about an hour to get the fire going and the stove hot. Then you have to feed the fire box periodically; too much coal and you smother it, too little and the heat goes down. Meanwhile, you have to shake the clinkers (burnt coal) out of the fire box occasionally or they cut off air circulation and the fire goes out. Of course, all this fire-tending is done while you're slicing, cutting, mixing and cooking.

Once the dishes start cooking "control" comes by moving pots and pans around. Over the fire box is hottest, the farther away from it, the (relatively) cooler it gets. We sometimes set our pots on inverted pie plates so whatever is in them doesn't cook too fast.

Then there's the oven. There's something about heat from coal that burns everything you try to bake. We overcome this by putting foil over our breads, cakes and other baked goods until they're almost done. Then we take the foil off and let them brown.

Everything prepared on a coal-fired stove is cooked "until it's done." I hate that

Part of the O'Brien*'s galley crew, left to right, Capt. Ed Lodigiani, Rich Vannucci, Jim Hallstrom, Joe Guzzetta, Mike Auen. Photo: Courtesy of Rich Vannucci.*

phrase when I see it in a cook book, but here you have no choice. We tried using an oven thermometer but they kept disappearing. In addition, what do you do if you want 350 degrees and the thermometer shows 300? Add more coal. Then it goes to 400. With time you learn to judge doneness by sight, taste, feel or probe (the old toothpick in the cake technique).

My first attempts on the *O'Brien*'s coal-fired stove were simple soups, stews, meats and fish. But I soon went in search of more exotic and challenging dishes — cream of peanut butter soup, apple dumplings, homemade bread and the like. Lately I've taken to recreating menus from old ships — real and fictional. We've done meals from the *Titanic*, Pacific Coast passenger ships, the Patrick O'Brian series and the Glencannon stories.

Meatloaf for 20 — or is it 40? One can never be sure how many will show up for dinner. Photo: author.

We have two galley crews on the ship — all volunteers. The one I'm on does the raffle prize dinners, recreating menus from historic ships for eight people. The ship's regular galley crew cooks lunch most weekends and volunteer work days and breakfast, lunch and dinner on special days such as steaming weekend and our annual cruises when a large volunteer group sleeps over. Their menus might not be as exotic as our raffle prize dinners, but the food is just as good. And their logistics are more challenging. We know exactly how many to prepare for but they cook for a larger group and never really know how many they're going to feed. People always show up unexpectedly, but they're never turned away — the *O'Brien* has always been known as "a good feeder." The galley crew's skill and attitude are admired and appreciated by everyone.

What follows are recipes from the menus we've recreated for the raffle prize dinners — the best fare from historic passenger liners, steamships, sailing ships, windjammers, tramps and freighters. Also included are some of the older, traditional recipes, such as hard tack, dandyfunk and a few others to keep them alive. We've included favorite recipes from the current *O'Brien* crew and a few other recipes just to round out some of the categories.

So sharpen your knives, tie on an apron and let the cooking begin!

One last thing. Don't worry about the coal. These recipes are all presented so you can use them on your gas or electric stove at home.

Eat hearty, mates!

Appetizers

Beginning a meal with *hors d'oeuvres* creates a sense of occasion. Whether it be shrimp cocktails, antipasti or canapes, an appetizer tells your guests that this meal is going to be more than ordinary.

Of course, when starting off with a taste-tempting opening course, one must be sure to do it right. Crackers, cheese and salami, while a good snack, won't do. Your guests deserve more than that. And, if you're like me, you want something more challenging. The fun comes two ways: for you in the preparation; for the guests in what they see before them and their enjoyment of its taste.

Blini and Caviar (zakuski)

The Glencannon stories appeared in the *Saturday Evening Post* during the 1930s, '40s and '50s. They featured a Scots chief engineer (Colin St. Andrew MacThrockle Glencannon) and his antics on board the British tramp, the SS *Inchcliffe Castle*.

One of the stories in the series dealt with the cook of the *Inchcliffe Castle* trading dinners with the cook of a Russian ship, the *Afansy Matushenko*. The Russian ship got steak and kidney pudding while the British ship ended up with blini and caviar, followed by borscht. Neither crew appreciated the change. Jessup, the *Inchcliffe*'s steward, tried to explain the new dish to his captain, "But they're really a very rare delicacy, sir. This 'ere black muck inside 'em that looks and smells like rancid buckshot is really genuwine surgeon's caviar, sir."

The *Inchcliffe Castle* was featured as the theme of one of our raffle prize dinners on the *Jeremiah O'Brien*. The first course was "folded-over pancakes" or *blini* served with caviar.

The *blini* are part of the traditional Russian appetizer known as *zakuski*. Basically, they are a buckwheat pancake served with melted butter and sour

The Inchcliffe Castle, *home to Coli Glencannon. The series has long been favorite among seafaring people. Curt Publishing Co.*

cream, topped with red and black caviar, smoked salmon or pickled herring.

Directions

Dissolve the yeast in ¼ C. lukewarm water. Combine it in a mixing bowl with the scalded milk. Stir in enough of the buckwheat flour, with the salt, to make a thick sponge. Cover and let rise in a warm place for about three hours.

Beat the egg yolks with the lukewarm milk, butter and sugar. Add the egg mixture to the sponge alternately with the remaining buckwheat flour. If the batter is not thin, add more milk. Beat well and let stand for about thirty minutes. Fold in the egg whites.

Pour enough batter on a hot, buttered griddle to form three-inch cakes. Cook, turning once.

To serve, place a dollop of sour cream on each blini and top with a teaspoon of caviar or a slice of smoked salmon or pickled herring. Fold each cake over once.

Serves 8.

Ingredients

1 pkg. yeast
1 C. milk, scalded and
    cooled to lukewarm
2 C. buckwheat flour
1 TBS. salt
3 egg yolks
1 C. lukewarm milk (not
    scalded)
1 TBS. melted butter
1 tsp. sugar
3 egg whites, beaten
    until stiff
caviar, smoked salmon
    and pickled herring
sour cream

Canapés à l'Amiral

The *Jeremiah O'Brien* has a special connection with the blockbuster movie *Titanic*. The engine room scenes for the movie were shot aboard our Liberty ship. By installing smaller versions of the engine room ladders and railings the ship's engine was made to appear much larger than it is. The *O'Brien* had a bad bearing at the time and in the movie you can even hear one of the bearings knocking if you know what to listen for.

With the popularity of the movie came a score of books, one of them *Last Dinner on the* Titanic by Rick Archbold and Dana McCauley. We used this as a point of departure for our own *Titanic* dinner which was a raffle prize from one of our cruises.

Dinner began with these canapés. This recipe is a bit complicated and time-consuming, but one I think is well worth while. The presentation is stunning and the taste superb.

Ingredients

½ thin baguette
1 tsp. lime juice
10 cooked shrimp,
 butterflied
Italian parsley
2 TBS. caviar

Directions

Shrimp Butter: In a skillet, heat oil over medium heat. Add shallot and garlic, cook, stirring frequently, for five minutes or until softened. Increase heat to high, add shrimp and sauté, stirring,

We served these on small, flat plates. Put a slice of butter lettuce on the plate and set the canapés on the lettuce. For some added color, include a slice of Italian tomato.

Shrimp Butter

1 TBS. vegetable oil
1 large minced shallot
1 clove minced garlic
8 oz. shrimp in shell
¼ C. brandy
4 oz. softened cream
  cheese
2 TBS. softened butter
1 TBS. tomato paste
¼ tsp. each salt and
  pepper
Dash vanilla

NOTES:
1) The vanilla is a nice touch here. It gives the dish an unexpected dimension. The "dash of vanilla" should be a healthy one. It's hard to use too much vanilla in anything.
2) Of course, the type of caviar depends on your budget. The appetizer will be good whether you use beluga or lumpfish.

for three to four minutes or until shrimp are pink and flesh opaque. (Watch this step closely or the shrimp will be tough and over-cooked). *Transfer mixture to food processor.*

Return pan to stove and pour in brandy; cook, stirring for thirty seconds or until brandy is reduced to glaze, scrape into shrimp mixture.

Purée shrimp mixture until finely chopped. Add cream cheese, butter, tomato paste, salt, pepper and vanilla. Process until smooth. Press mixture through coarse sieve set over a bowl and discard shells.

Slice baguette into 20 thin slices. Place on baking sheet and toast under broiler for one minute on each side or until lightly golden. Reserve.

Drizzle lime juice over cooked shrimp halves; stir and reserve.

Place shrimp butter in pastry bag fitted with star tube. Pipe shrimp butter onto toasts. Top with cooked butterflied shrimp half and a parsley leaf. Top each canapé with an equal amount of caviar.

Makes 20.

Crackerhash

This is a nineteenth century sailing ship dish. Bear in mind the fare on the average windjammer consisted of hard tack and salt beef or salt pork and little else. After a couple of months, anything different tasted good! It's included simply in the interest of keeping alive some of the old seafaring recipes.

Directions

Break the hard tack into small pieces, mix with the salt beef and oil. Form into cracker shapes about 1/8 inch thick. Bake in a 350°F. oven for thirty minutes or until the meat is cooked.

Serves 4.

Ingredients

½ lb. hard tack (recipe on p. 10), broken in small pieces
½ lb. salt beef, diced
2 TBS. vegetable oil

Curried Cheese and Chutney Dip

Ingredients

8 oz. softened Philadelphia cream cheese
1 C. sharp cheddar cheese
1 tsp. curry powder
3 TBS. sherry
8 oz. mango chutney
1/2 C. chopped green onions (scallions)

NOTE:
When chopping scallions, cut the white part in thin slices, then as you reach the green/white part, cut in increasingly large pieces until they are about ½ inch at the green end.

One of our raffle prize dinners was a tribute to the *Cotton Blossom* from the musical "Showboat" and this appetizer was included in their souvenir, *The Showboat Cook Book*, by June Jackson.

Based on Mississippi River steamboat cooking, this dish is an unusually delectable combination of flavors. The key must be the cream cheese. I can't think of a recipe that has cream cheese in it that isn't popular. This is the kind of dish that people taste first out of curiosity, then, the second time because it is so good and they want to try figuring out what is in it. The third time is to get some more before it's all gone.

Directions

Mix the cream cheese and the cheddar. Add the curry powder and sherry. Form in a mound on a serving dish. Pour the chutney over the cheese and sprinkle the onions on top. Serve with Ritz crackers.

Deviled Eggs Masterson

One of the menus we did was based on the passenger liner *Lurline*, a favorite for decades among those traveling between San Francisco and the Hawaiian Islands from the 1930s to the 1960s. It was five days and four nights each way — a leisurely and relaxing way to travel. Our raffle prize dinner was based on the New Year's Eve dinner served on board that wonderful old ship on December 31, 1957.

Eggs have gotten a lot of bad press in recent years because of cholesterol. At this writing it appears there was a lot of hysteria involved in the earlier findings, and it's now agreed that four or more eggs a week cause no harm at all. Something to do with the way the natural ingredients of an egg are assimilated into the system. So don't feel anxious about having a couple of these before dinner.

Bev Masterson always sets up the officers' mess as if it were the first class dining room on one of the fabled passenger liners of the past. Photo: Bev Masterson.

Directions

Cut a dozen hard-cooked eggs lengthwise and remove the yolks.

Force six of the yolks through a fine sieve with ¼ C. cooked fish, 1 tsp. prepared mustard and enough mayonnaise to make a firm paste. Season to taste with cayenne and curry powder. Stuff twelve of the egg white halves using

Ingredients

12 hard-cooked eggs
¼ C. cooked fish,
   salmon or cod
3 TBS. pâté de foie gras
1 tsp. prepared mustard
mayonnaise
cayenne
curry powder
capers
truffle
chervil
parsley
salt
pepper

Dinner ABOARD S.S. **LURLINE**

COMMODORE H. R. GILLESPIE, USNR, *Commanding*
CAPTAIN VERNON A. JOHNSON, USNR, *Staff Captain*

Tuesday, December 31, 1957

APPETIZERS

Chilled Hearts of Celery
Fresh Prawns Cocktail
Imported Italian Antipasto
Iced Tomato Juice or Guava Nectar
Fresh Papaya Cocktail Creme de Menthe

Green and Ripe Olives
Stuffed Eggs, Virginia
Hawaiian Poi Cocktail
Croustades Raw Meat, Tartare
French Sardines in Olive Oil

SOUPS

Consomme with Vermicelli
Chilled Tomato Bouillon
Cream of Chicken, Marie Louise

FISH

Hawaiian Opakapaka Saute, Brown Lemon Butter, Cole Slaw Salad
Poached Black Cod, Hollandaise Sauce, Parsley Potato

ENTREES

Chicken Saute Mascote, Artichoke, Mushrooms, Noisette Potatoes, Fines Herbes
Assorted Garden Fresh Vegetable Platter with Poached Egg
Smoked Loin of Pork, Sauce Piquante, Lady Apple
Homemade Ravioli a la Italienne au Gratin
To Order from Our Charcoal Broiler (Allow Ten Minutes)
Broiled Jumbo Squab on Croustade, Currant Jelly, Waffle Potatoes

ROASTS

Roast Prime Ribs of Beef au Jus, Hot Corn Bread, Creamed Horseradish

VEGETABLES---POTATOES

Zucchini Saute
Baked Idaho Potato

Buttered White Turnips, Persillade
Maitre d'Hotel

Kernel Corn Saute
Roast

Carolina Rice
Saratoga Chips

COLD BUFFET

Homemade Headcheese, Sauce Vinaigrette, Vegetable Salad
Cold Sliced Cured Smoked Turkey, Waldorf Salad

SALADS---DRESSINGS

Sliced Tomato Salad
Tossed Green Salad
French   Lemon   Mayonnaise   Thousand Island

Florida Fruit Salad
Hearts of Lettuce
Roquefort   Garlic

DESSERTS

Coupe Rose Marie   Macaroon Layer Cake   Cherry Tartlet   Petits Fours   Vanilla Ice Cream
Chocolate Souffle Pudding, Fruit Sauce   Raspberry Sherbet   Compote of Fruit

CHEESE

Monterey Jack   Imported Swiss   Camembert   Cheddar   Philadelphia   Edam
Rye-Krisp, Melba Toast, Saltines or Water Crackers

BEVERAGES

Coffee   Milk   Sanka   Chocolate
Green or Orange Pekoe Tea

Demi Tasse Served in Smoking Room

Matson Lines

Consult the Wine List for a selection exactly to your taste.

J. M. ABRAMSON, *Chief Steward*   ANGELO FUSETTI, *Executive Chef*

NOTES:
**1) Be careful on the cayenne, a little bit goes a long way.
2) On the other hand, be generous with the curry powder; it greatly enhances the taste.**

a pastry bag fitted with a small fancy tube.

Mash six hard-cooked egg yolks with 3 TBS. pâté de foie gras, some chopped chervil and salt and pepper to taste. Stuff the remaining twelve egg white halves using a pastry bag fitted with a small fancy tube. Sprinkle with a little finely chopped truffle and parsley. Top with a sprinkling of capers.

We served these as part of an antipasto tray and together they set an elegant tone for the dinner to follow.

Hard Tack

Even hard tack requires a properly stoked stove. Author adding more coal to the fire. S. Rose.

This seagoing staple dates back several centuries. It was common on sailing ships worldwide. Packed in barrels, it lasted for years and at a time when food preservation was almost nonexistent, it was standard in seagoing cuisine. It's included here because it wouldn't be right to have a cookbook based on shipboard cooking without it.

Directions

Preheat the oven to 325°F. Stir the flour and salt together. Add the water, stirring, until you have a very stiff dough. Turn onto a floured surface, cover with a damp towel and let rest for ten minutes. Knead the dough for a minute or two until all the flour is absorbed. With a rolling pin, roll out to about ½ inch thick. Fold the dough over on itself several times and repeat the process. Continue until smooth and elastic, about thirty minutes. Roll the dough into a rectangle about ½ inch thick and cut into 2-inch squares or rounds. Prick the biscuits with a fork or toothpick. Place on a cookie sheet and bake for one hour. Cool on racks.

For a true seagoing experience, place in jars or tins for several months. Check periodically for weevils. Knock weevils out before eating.

Ingredients

4 C. flour
1 tsp. salt
1 to 1½ C. water

VARIATIONS:
1. Add 2 tsp. butter to make more palatable.
2. Before baking, mist the hard tack with water and sprinkle with rock salt.
3. After cooking ten minutes, sprinkle with fresh grated parmesan cheese and chopped fresh parsley.
4. Before baking, brush lightly with butter and sprinkle with cinnamon and sugar.

Prosciutto and Melon

When passenger ships actually went somewhere rather than "cruising to nowhere" as they do now, they frequently had theme dinners to vary the menu. They might have a "Tokyo" night or a "Parisian Dinner" or sometimes a special "Captain's Dinner" which was unusually lavish. On December 28, 1957 the luxury Matson liner SS *Lurline* featured an "Italian Night." Using that as a basis, we replicated the *Lurline* menu on a more modest scale for one of our raffle prize dinners. The first course for our Italian Night was prosciutto and melon. This is one of those dishes that is simple to put together, yet tastes wonderful.

Ingredients

1 ripe cantaloupe
8 slices prosciutto

NOTES:
1) For the best flavor it is essential that the melon be soft and ripe, not hard.
2) Although domestic prosciutto will work, I'd recommend the imported Italian product. It's not that much more expensive and the flavor is far better.

Directions

Cut the melon in half. Remove the seeds. Cut each half in four half-moon shapes. Remove the rind. Wrap each piece of melon with one slice of prosciutto.

Serves 8.

Roasted Chili Pecans

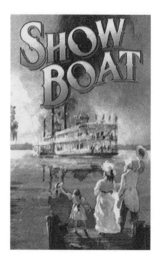

The classic Broadway musical "Showboat" is the quintessential American story. When it was revived and toured the country a few years ago one of the stops was San Francisco. Among the items sold in the lobby during intermission was *The Showboat Cookbook.* It was full of riverboat recipes that tantalized the imagination and I couldn't rest until we created one of our raffle prize dinners on a Showboat theme. The recipes have been modified, but they might have been served on the *Cotton Blossom,* the boat from the musical. We started off with Roasted Chili Pecans, an unusual dish when you are used to having pecans at the end of the meal in pies, candies and desserts.

Directions

Melt the butter in a cast iron skillet. Add everything else except the pecans and mix. Add the pecans. Stir over low heat until the nuts start to brown. Remove from heat and spread on a greased baking sheet. Roast at 200°F. for twenty to thirty minutes.

Makes 2 cups.

Ingredients

¼ C. butter
1 TBS. Worcestershire sauce
1 tsp. Tabasco sauce
1 tsp. salt
¼ tsp. cayenne
3/4 tsp. chili powder
2 C. pecan halves

NOTE:
Watch the nuts closely while they're roasting. If they start to burn, they will do so very quickly. In fact, the night we did this in our coal-fired stove we had trouble with the heat in the oven and had to make a second batch (which also burned), then cull the burnt ones out of both batches to make one two-cup serving of good nuts. (Working with this stove, we have learned to keep extra ingredients on hand!)

NATIONAL LIBERTY SHIP MEMORIAL

~ SS JEREMIAH O'BRIEN ~

MENU
Saturday, February 27, 1999

River Bottom Roasted Pecans
Curried Cheese and Chutney Spread with Crackers

Creole Shrimp Gumbo

Crawfish Etoufee

Roast Pork Tenderloin

Wild Rice-Pecan Dressing

Buttermilk Biscuits

Lower Mississippi Delta Country Chess Pie
Downriver Chocolate Cake
Coffee

Based on the Broadway musical SHOWBOAT
Dinner aboard the paddle wheel steamer *Cotton Blossom*
at the turn of the 20th Century

This was the menu we presented to our raffle prize winners for the Showboat dinner.

Shrimp Cocktail

Crab Cocktail
For a great crab cocktail, substitute 1-1½ lb. of fresh crabmeat for the shrimp in this recipe and use the same sauce.

Sometimes the simplest things are the best. It's hard to beat a good shrimp cocktail. Just enough shrimp to whet the appetite, a good sauce and you have a dish that pleases the eye, tantalizes the nose and tastes fantastic. We've served this as a first course on several of our *O'Brien* dinners.

Directions

Put enough water in a pot or large saucepan to more than cover the shrimp (but don't put the shrimp in yet). Add salt. Bring water to boil. Add shrimp and boil until color changes and shrimp are just done (about 5 minutes or less). Don't overcook the shrimp or they'll get tough and lose their flavor. *Pour off hot water and let shrimp cool.*

Prepare the sauce by mixing together the catsup, horseradish, Worcestershire and lemon juice. Adjust mixture to personal taste. Peel the shrimp. Arrange decoratively on a leaf of butter lettuce on a small plate or in a stemmed glass. Drizzle sauce on thick part of shrimp.

Serves 8.

Ingredients

40 large shrimp or prawns, unpeeled, uncooked
salt
water

Sauce
½ C. catsup
2 TBS. horseradish
2 tsp. Worcestershire sauce
1 TBS. lemon juice
butter lettuce for garnish

NOTES:
**1) Be creative in boiling the shrimp. There are probably as many recipes for this as there are Cajuns in Louisiana. Start with a couple of tablespoons of salt. Add any one, any combination or all of the following: peppercorns, bay leaf, thyme, tarragon, allspice, dill weed. You can also get "shrimp boil" at most markets, which will give the shrimp a good flavor.
2) For the sauce, be brave, add more horseradish or throw in a few dashes of Tabasco, adjust the balance to your own likes and taste.**

The sailing board was posted for departure at noon on April 18, 1994. So began our historic five-month voyage to Normandy. Photo: Author.

Time Capsule

The Normandy Voyage

The *Jeremiah O'Brien*'s epic return to Normandy in 1994 for the 50th Anniversary of D-Day was truly "the voyage of a lifetime." For many it brought back memories of earlier Liberty ships; for others it was a new experience. The galley and its coal-fired stove were very much a part of the daily experience, as the crew quickly found after departing San Francisco.

It wasn't long before we realized there are actually some advantages to sailing an old Liberty ship over modern ones. Modern ships are air-conditioned, all the rooms, passageways and entrances have airtight doors. There are no smells outside your own room. On the O'Brien, the doors aren't sealed. They have louvers at the bottom and portholes are left open for ventilation and every time the cooks began working in the galley the smell of food permeated the ship. It was wonderful, the mixed smells of chocolate chip cookies, bacon, bread, pancakes, sausage, chicken, more cookies, roasts, potatoes, muffins and more cookies. Even the simple pungent smell of coal burning somehow added to the feeling of traveling back in history to a better time.

Appointment in Normandy (1995)
Walter W. Jaffee

Swordfish Fritters

One of the dinners we did on the SS *Jeremiah O'Brien* was based on the Aubrey/Maturin novels of Patrick O'Brian. This series is a favorite with seafarers, ranking right up there with Forrester's Hornblower series. When the companion cookbook for the Patrick O'Brian novels, *Lobscouse and Spotted Dog*, by Anne Chotzinoff Grossman and Lisa Grossman Thomas, came out it seemed a natural for the nautical dinners we featured on board. Of course, we had to adapt the recipes to our coal-fired stove.

We started the dinner with Swordfish Fritters, an unusual and very tasty appetizer.

Ingredients

2 lb. swordfish, skin removed
3 C. lard or oil for deep-frying
2 eggs
1 TBS. melted butter
1 C. flour
1 tsp. salt
2/3 C. cold water

Directions

Cut the swordfish into 1-inch cubes. Pat them dry.

In a heavy saucepan or deep-fryer, heat oil to about 370°F.

Whisk the eggs until frothy and add the melted butter. Stir in the flour and salt. Gradually add the water, whisking until the batter is smooth.

Dip a few pieces of swordfish in the batter, turning them so that they are coated on all sides. Drop them gently into the hot oil, stir briefly to make sure they

NOTE:
A good sauce for this is: 1 C. mayonnaise, 1 tsp. Tabasco, 1 TBS. lemon juice, combined.

do not stick together, and fry until golden brown. Remove with a slotted spoon, drain briefly and keep warm. Repeat with remaining fish.

Serves 8 as a first course.

We served these on lettuce leaves with a dab of the sauce on the side. It was an attractive dish and disappeared quickly.

Cooking at sea has changed a bit since the British Navy of the 1700s, left. We no longer work on the open deck, but the equipment doesn't seem to be that much different.Left, National Maritime Museum, Greenwich, England.

It's the nature of volunteer work that everyone helps out. Below, Rich Vannucci (with super-sized ladle) at the steam kettle we sometimes use for very large batches of soup. Photo: S. Rose.

Above, Bev Masterson handles a smaller portion on the galley range. The mitts are necessary because of the intense heat radiating from the stove. Right, the author in a rare moment of relaxation while the soup simmers. Paddles over his left shoulder are for stirring large kettles of soup and stew. Photos: S. Rose.

Soups

A good "head of steam" shows this kettle of salted water is ready for lobsters. With an unregulated coal fire, you have to keep close watch that the liquid doesn't boil off (too much heat) or stop simmering (too little heat). Photo: author.

More than anything else, soup can be considered a one-dish meal. Whether it be an Italian minestrone loaded with vegetables and topped with grated cheese or a French bouillabaisse packed with clams, mussels, lobster and fish or a Louisiana bayou gumbo, soup has everything. Flavors, textures, aroma and appearance meld to form the perfect dish.

Good soup can be similar to perpetual motion, just going on forever. In fact, one of the favorite dishes among the crew on President Roosevelt's yacht *Potomac* was a dish called "perpetual soup." The cooks kept a pot on the back of the stove to which they simply added a little liquid and whatever leftovers were on hand. The resulting broth changed character from week to week according to whether FDR's menu included oysters, turkey, beef or even hot dogs. The surviving crewmembers talk about it to this day.

What follows does not include perpetual soup, but there are a lot of other good recipes I'm sure you will enjoy.

Bisque de Homard

A good bisque takes a lot of work and close attention to detail but is well worth it. I've never met a bisque I didn't like. We served this one at our "Patrick O'Brian Dinner" and there wasn't a drop left afterwards.

Directions

Plunge the lobsters about five minutes into boiling water, or until bright red. Remove the claws and legs. Separate the tails from the bodies.

In a large stewpot, melt 3 tablespoons of the butter. Add the onion and carrot and sauté until the onion is transparent. Add the parsley, thyme and bay leaf.

Add the lobster and cook over medium heat, turning the pieces frequently, until the shells are deep red on all sides. Warm ¼ C. brandy, set it aflame and pour it over the lobster. After the flames have died down, add the wine and 1 C. of the stock. Cover, bring to a boil, reduce heat, and simmer twenty to twenty-five minutes.

Remove the lobsters and let them cool. Remove the vegetables from the cooking liquid; reserve both the vegetables and the liquid.

Ingredients

4 live lobsters, about 1½ lbs. each
11 TBS. butter
1 small onion, peeled and diced
1 carrot, peeled and diced
Small handful of fresh parsley
Small handful of fresh thyme
1 bay leaf
½ C. brandy
½ C. dry white wine
5-6 C. fish stock or court bouillon (recipe on p. 86)
2 TBS. dry sherry
4 C. milk
3/4 C. flour
¼ C. heavy cream

We did this in a very large pot on the *O'Brien's* coal-fired stove. Possibly because of the difficulty in controlling the heat, too much boiled off and there wasn't enough liquid remaining after the simmer for twelve people. I'd suggest having an extra four cups of fish stock on hand in case you have the same difficulty. Simply add the stock after you return the soup to the pot until you have the quantity you want.

Pick the meat from the shells. Crush the shells and set aside. Dice the meat finely, reserving a few big rosy pieces for garnish. Sprinkle the meat with the sherry and set aside.

Pour the milk and 4 C. of the remaining stock into the pot and bring it to a boil. Meanwhile, melt 6 TBS. of the butter in a small saucepan. Add the flour, stir well, and cook over low heat until the flour is completely absorbed. Reduce the heat under the soup. Add the roux to the soup and stir until slightly thickened. Add the crushed shells and the cooked vegetables, along with the reserved cooking liquid. Simmer, covered, 1½ hours.

Strain the soup through a very fine mesh and return it to the pot. Thin if necessary with the remaining stock. Add the cream, the remaining brandy and butter and the lobster meat. Cook until the butter is melted and the lobster heated through. Serve with a loaf of crusty French bread and a salad.

Serves 6 as an entrée, 12 as a soup course.

Borscht

This is a traditional Russian dish. Because it has a reputation of being peasant food, it is often overlooked. Don't be fooled. Borscht is a great tasting soup and one you'll try more than once.

We did a dinner based on the Glencannon stories by Guy Gilpatric that appeared in the old *Saturday Evening Post*. Our raffle prize winners were presented with a menu from the English tramp steamer SS *Inchcliffe Castle*. Based on meals mentioned throughout the stories, it was a great hit with our guests. Why a Russian dish on a British ship? Well, in one story the *Inchcliffe Castle* was tied up to a dock next to a Russian ship and the cooks of each ship decided to trade dinners one evening. Part of the plot dealt with racing cockroaches, but you'll have to read the story to find out about *that*.

Ingredients

1 small head of cabbage, cored, sliced thinly
1 medium onion, chopped
2 C. chopped fresh vine-ripened tomatoes (or 16 oz. canned stewed tomatoes)
2 C. peeled, diced fresh beets (or 16 oz. canned sliced beets)
2 C. beef broth
salt
pepper
¼ C. olive oil
Sour cream for garnish

Directions

Saute the onion and the cabbage in the oil until softened slightly. Add tomatoes, beets, beef broth, salt and pepper. Cover, bring to a boil over medium high heat. Reduce heat to low and simmer for one hour. Once the soup is done purée it in batches in a blender. Serve with a dollop of sour cream on top. Serves 8.

NOTES:
1. Hothouse tomatoes aren't worth wasting your time with.
2. If you can get fresh beets, they add a lot of color and flavor to the dish.

Cabbage and Ham Soup

Our Navy volunteer cooks brought this recipe with them and, according to Rich Vannucci, it quickly became a favorite with the *O'Brien* crew. Cabbage is often overlooked as an ingredient in soups, but here it comes into its own. And, of course, you can't go wrong when you have ham in a recipe.

Ingredients

¼ C. green bell pepper, diced
¼ C. celery, diced
½ C. onion, diced
3 TBS. parsley
3 TBS. butter
2 C. cooked ham, diced
1 bay leaf
2 TBS. flour
1 TBS. chicken stock concentrate
3 C. cold water
2 C. cabbage, finely chopped
1 TBS. water
1 C. sour cream

Directions

In a large frying pan, cook the green pepper, celery, onion and parsley in 2 TBS. of the butter over medium heat until they are soft, but not browned. Add the ham and bay leaf. Cook until the ham is heated through. Blend together the flour, chicken stock concentrate and 3 C. of cold water and pour into the pan with the ham. Bring to a boil over high heat, stirring, and simmer a minute or two. Pour into a soup kettle to keep warm. In the same frying pan, melt the remaining 1 TBS. of butter over high heat, add the cabbage and 1 TBS. of water. Cook, stirring until the cabbage turns brighter in color and softens slightly. Mix into the soup. Serve with a large spoonful of sour cream in each serving.

Serves 4.

Crawfish Bisque

Some of the best cooking in the United States developed along the Mississippi River, in particular around New Orleans with its French and Cajun influences. Buried in my files was a menu for a paddlewheeler that ran in the 1930s named the *Creole Queen* and she became the focus of our "New Orleans Night" for this dinner, one of our raffle prize dinners on the *O'Brien*.

Crawfish are a lot of trouble to cook and work with and a lot of trouble to eat. But they eat so good! And the dish looks and smells great. This is one of the best smelling, tasting and appearing dishes you can make. The time and effort involved is well worth it. Try this recipe once, and I guarantee you'll frequently be asked to do it again.

Directions

Make the roux. In a large five to six quart kettle, melt the bacon drippings over low heat. Gradually add the flour, stirring constantly, and cook over low heat until a medium brown roux the color of peanut butter is formed. It's important to the flavoring that it get that brown.

Meanwhile, melt the butter in a skillet and brown the chopped onion and white

Ingredients

The Roux
5 TBS. bacon drippings
1 C. flour

The Base
2 TBS. butter (salted or unsalted works equally well)
1 C. chopped onion
¼ C. chopped scallions (the white part only)
3 TBS. green scallion tops, thinly sliced
2 ½ TBS. celery tops
2 TBS. fresh parsley, chopped
1 TBS. minced garlic
½ C. chopped crawfish tails (about 2 dozen tails)
¼ C. crawfish fat
1½ C. whole crawfish tails

Liquid and Seasonings
2 qt. cold water
1 TBS. salt
¼ tsp. freshly ground black pepper
½ tsp. cayenne
2 whole bay leaves, crumbled
1 tsp. dried thyme
4 whole cloves
12 whole allspice
½ tsp. mace

Garnish
2-3 doz. stuffed crawfish
heads or 1 lb. tails
2 doz. whole crawfish

NOTES:
1. My original recipe suggests substituting lard for the bacon drippings, but don't you dare. The bacon fat is one more layer of flavor in a multi-flavored dish.
2. Many southern recipes call for shallots and usually they mean scallions. It's just a regional name for what the rest of us might call green onions or scallions.
3. Crawfish fat is a bit hard to come by. Usually, if you start with the whole creature you can get some fat out of the head. But it takes a lot of extra work to boil several dozen of the critters, reserve some for the tails, and take the fat out of the heads. I'd recommend getting prepackaged crawfish tails (already out of the shell, what a great labor saving device!) and whole crawfish. That way you can use the whole ones for garnish and for their tails as above, but you can substitute the prepackaged ones for the chopped tails above. Substitute some more bacon drippings for the crawfish fat if you don't have any.
4. For extra zing, you can safely put as much as a full tsp. of pepper and a full tsp. of cayenne in the liquid.

parts of the scallions. When the onion mixture is browned turn off the heat and let them sit. When the roux reaches the desired color, add the contents of the skillet, stirring rapidly, then add the scallion tops, the celery, parsley, garlic and all the seasonings. Mix thoroughly. Add the ½ C. chopped crawfish meat and the crawfish fat and mix.

Keeping the heat low, very gradually add the water, stirring constantly to keep the mixture smooth. Raise the heat to high and bring the bisque to a boil, then lower the heat to simmer. After fifteen minutes of simmering, add the whole crawfish tails and simmer an additional forty-five minutes. Five minutes before serving, add two to three dozen stuffed crawfish heads or one pound of crawfish tails. To really make it look good, throw in a couple of dozen whole crawfish. *Serve in large bowls. Boiled rice may be added.*

If there's any left over, (that's never happened at our house), you can refrigerate it, then heat it before serving. Don't bring it to a boil as this will overcook the crawfish.

Serves 8.

Cheese and Corn Chowder

This is another Navy recipe popular with the *O'Brien*'s crew, supplied by Rich Vannucci with one change. The original dish calls for frozen corn. I suggest using fresh white corn when available. It's much more tasty and has more substance — you get that "tooth action" that is usually missing in frozen vegetables.

Directions

Bring potatoes, water, bouillon, cayenne and black pepper to boil over high heat in a large saucepan. Reduce heat to medium, cover and simmer for ten minutes or until potatoes are tender. Stir in 2½ C. of the milk and the corn. In a small bowl stir together the remaining ½ C. milk and the flour. Stir into the potato mixture. Cook until slightly thickened and bubbly. Add cheese and stir until melted. Spoon into bowls and top with parsley.

Serves 4.

Ingredients

**3 medium potatoes,
   skin on, diced
1 C. water
1 cube chicken bouillon
1/8 tsp. cayenne
pepper to taste
3 C. milk
1½ C. white corn, about
   four ears worth
2 TBS. flour
6 oz. cheddar cheese,
   grated
1 TBS. parsley, chopped**

NOTE:
To remove the kernels from an ear of corn, simply slice them off with a sharp knife, cutting lengthwise from about halfway up the ear to the end. When the kernels are off half the ear, reverse and repeat. This will give you several rows of sliced kernels. Cut crosswise into medium dice.

Considering how simple the ingredients are, this is a surprisingly good dish. Our dinner guests wanted seconds.

Cream of Barley

Ingredients

1 TBS. vegetable oil
1/4 C. finely chopped salt
  pork or bacon
2 chopped carrots
2 chopped onions
3 cloves minced garlic
1 bay leaf
2 tsp. parsley
1/4 tsp. peppercorns
1 C. pearl barley
7 C. beef stock
1 C. whipping cream
2 TBS. whiskey
1 TBS. red wine vinegar
Salt and pepper

NOTES:
1. Bacon works better than salt pork. It gives the soup just a hint of smoke flavor, and since the soup is not strongly flavored to begin with, blends well.
2. Generally, vegetables needn't be chopped too finely. Usually I'll cut them in about half-inch pieces. They get soft anyway and if you purée the soup it won't matter what size they are.
3. You can use more parsley and peppercorns than called for if you wish to give the soup a little more character.

We served this as part of our *Titanic* dinner. To avoid the possibility of jinxing anything, we dated the menu as coming from two days before the disaster. No sense in tempting fate when you're aboard ship. The recipe is a variation of that found in *Last Dinner on the Titanic*.

Directions

In a large pot, heat oil over medium heat; add salt pork or bacon and cook, stirring often, for two minutes. Stir in carrot, onion, and garlic, cover and cook, stirring occasionally, for ten minutes or until vegetables are very soft.

Meanwhile, make a bouquet garni of the bay leaf, parsley and peppercorns wrapped in cheesecloth. Stir barley into vegetable mixture, cook stirring, for about forty-five seconds. Pour in stock and add the bouquet garni. Bring to a boil. Reduce the heat to low and simmer, covered, for forty to forty-five minutes or until the barley is tender.

Remove from heat; purée in batches until almost smooth. Transfer to a clean pot; cook over medium heat until steaming. Remove from heat and whisk in cream, whiskey and vinegar. Season with salt and pepper.

Makes 6 to 8 servings.

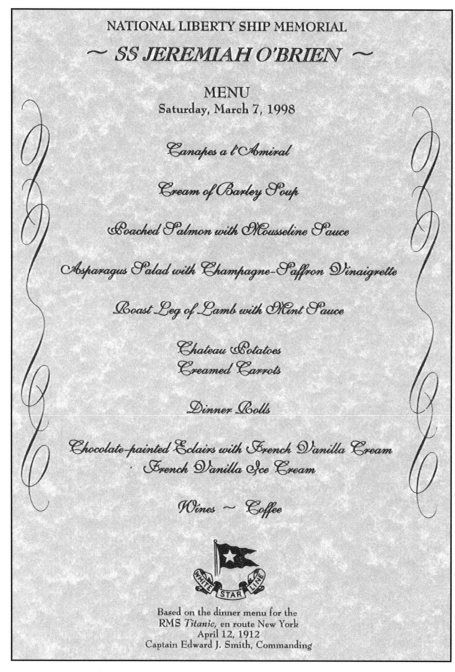

NATIONAL LIBERTY SHIP MEMORIAL

~ *SS JEREMIAH O'BRIEN* ~

MENU
Saturday, March 7, 1998

Canapes a l'Amiral

Cream of Barley Soup

Poached Salmon with Mousseline Sauce

Asparagus Salad with Champagne-Saffron Vinaigrette

Roast Leg of Lamb with Mint Sauce

Chateau Potatoes
Creamed Carrots

Dinner Rolls

Chocolate-painted Eclairs with French Vanilla Cream
French Vanilla Ice Cream

Wines ~ Coffee

Based on the dinner menu for the
RMS *Titanic*, en route New York
April 12, 1912
Captain Edward J. Smith, Commanding

In creating our Titanic *dinner we dated it two days before the fabled disaster so as not to jinx anything.*

S.S. President Roosevelt

CAPTAIN RALPH O. WILSON, Commanding

PRESENTS

Arabian Nights

Selamat, Hamdu li Jlah 'ala 1-Salamat
(Greetings and praised be Allah for your safety)

Inna Li-Iah Wa Inna Ileihi Ragi'oun
(To Allah we belong and to Him wearily we return)

WORLD CRUISE, VOYAGE 50

En Route MOMBASA, KENYA-EAST, THURSDAY MARCH 6, 1969

This menu cover comes from the President Roosevelt *during the days of her around-the-world service. Author's collection.*

Cream of Tomato

Owned by American President Lines, the President Roosevelt *provided around-the-world passenger ship service in the 1950s and 1960s. Photo: American President Lines.*

This soup was featured on the passenger liner *President Roosevelt* in its around-the-world service in 1968. Capt. Ralph Wilson was captain of that voyage. Interestingly, he was later one of the masters of the *Jeremiah O'Brien* after she became a museum ship. It seemed thoroughly appropriate to feature a dinner from one of his earlier commands as a raffle prize dinner.

Tomato soup is normally rather ordinary and a staple of almost every diner and eatery along America's highways. But this recipe elevates that simple dish to the gourmet level. The difference is fresh vine-ripened tomatoes and a

Ingredients

2 qts. chicken broth
6 large vine-ripened tomatoes, chopped
4 C. canned tomato purée
1 clove garlic, minced
8 white peppercorns
1 TBS. sugar
1 C. cream
1 TBS. butter

touch of garlic. The result is a rich, bright red broth that looks good, smells wonderful and tastes superb. And the recipe is very simple.

Directions

In a soup kettle mix the broth, tomatoes, purée, garlic, peppercorns and sugar. Cook for two hours. Add cream and butter.

Serves 8.

Fasolatha (Greek Bean Soup)

Seafarers travel the world and in their travels sample foods that landlubbers may not know about. This recipe comes from Rich Vannucci, one of the *O'Brien*'s galley crew, who retired from the Navy. He says it is the national soup of Greece.

Directions

Bring beans to boil over high heat. Reduce to low and simmer, covered, for one hour. Remove from water and drain. Using same pot the beans were cooked in, sauté the onions, garlic, salt and pepper in olive oil. When vegetables are soft, add tomatoes. Cook five minutes, add oregano and hot water. Then add beans, salt pork and bring to a boil over medium heat. Reduce heat to low and simmer for one-half hour. Add celery and carrots. Simmer one-half hour.

Serves 12

Ingredients

1 lb. small white navy beans
3 oz. salt pork, cut into small pieces
2 medium onions, coarsely chopped
6 cloves garlic
4 diced fresh tomatoes
1 TBS. oregano
salt & pepper
4 stalks celery
six carrots, in medium slices
olive oil
1 gal. hot water

Note:
This soup gets better when refrigerated and reheated the next day.

AMERICAN PRESIDENT LINES

PRESENTS

INTERNATIONAL NIGHT

ABOARD THE

S. S. President Roosevelt
CAPTAIN RALPH G. WILSON, Commanding

Ingredients

4 large onions
¼ C. butter
1 TBS. flour
1½ qt. beef broth
French bread
Gruyère cheese, grated

NOTES:
**1. In our part of California we get large, sweet red onions in the spring which are ideal for this, although yellow onions work as well.
2. It's important to use good French bread (sour dough is perfect) and quality cheese.**

French Onion Soup

The *President Roosevelt* was known for her around-the-world service, one of the few passenger liners that ever sailed that route on a regular basis. As might be expected, her menus were cosmopolitan, featuring dishes from every country along the way. One of our raffle prize dinners included dishes from several menus, a truly international meal. After a prawn cocktail appetizer, we served French onion soup, which was based on the following recipe, the best I've ever found for this classic dish.

Directions

Peel and thinly slice the onions, separating the rings. In a large saucepan sauté the onions in the butter over very low heat. Stir with a wooden spoon until they are an even golden brown. Sprinkle with the flour, stir until blended and add the beef broth. Bring heat to medium high and stir until soup begins to boil. Reduce heat to low and simmer for about twenty minutes.

Meanwhile, place a toasted round of French bread in each serving bowl and heap with grated cheese. Add soup. Serve with toasted rounds of bread and a bowl of grated cheese on the side.

Serves 8.

Hotch Potch

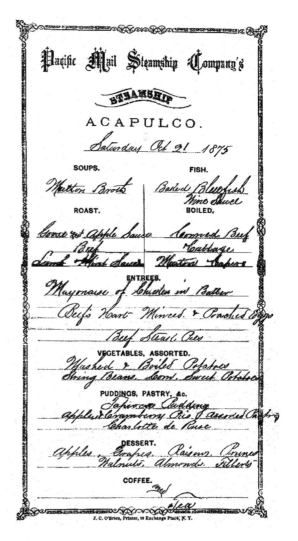

In recreating ships' menus for our raffle prize dinners we've noticed that the older the menu the simpler it was, in the sense that they usually had fewer dishes listed. But that didn't mean they were boring. Some of those early shipboard dinners featured interesting fare, occasionally with some very pleasant surprises. This one started out as "mutton broth" from a menu belonging to the Pacific Mail Steamer *Acapulco* which ran a passenger service on the West Coast in the late 1800s. The original dinner was

Ingredients

1½ lb. chopped lamb
  meat
olive oil
1½ C. green peas
2/3 C. fava or lima
  beans
6 green onions,
  chopped
2 carrots, peeled and
  chopped
3/4 lb. turnips, peeled
  and chopped
1 medium cauliflower
1 small head lettuce
salt
10 C. water
1 tsp. chopped parsley

NOTE:
1. You can use any cut
of meat, even stew, neck
or brisket. Leave the
bones in for extra
flavor, but take them
out before serving.
2. A not-well-known
trick for good soups and
stews is to briefly stir-
fry all meats and veg-
etables in a little oil or
butter first. This cara-
melizes natural sugars
and intensifies the
flavors.

served on October 21, 1875. With a few
variations, we served the same thing 123
years later on the *Jeremiah O'Brien.*

Directions

*Trim the meat and stir-fry briefly in
olive oil, turning frequently. Then put it
in a pan with the water and some salt.
Bring to a boil and skim the surface. Add
half the peas, all the beans, onions,
carrots and turnips. Simmer for one
hour.*

*Meanwhile, trim the cauliflower and
break it into small florets. Shred the
lettuce. After the soup has simmered for
an hour, add the rest of the peas, the
cauliflower and the lettuce and simmer
for an additional thirty minutes. Check
for seasoning, stir in the parsley and
serve.*

Serves 6 to 8.

This is one of those recipes that
surprises. The ingredients are simple, yet
the final result is quite stunning — a
terrific soup, especially good for a cold
day. The key is to use fresh ingredients.

J.O.B. (Jeremiah O'Brien) Lentil Soup

Joe Guzzetta is a member of the ship's galley crew. He also made part of the *O'Brien*'s great voyage to Normandy in 1994, lending his fine talents in the steward's department. Joe has a few recipes of his own which are extremely popular with the crew. Many of the ship's volunteers look forward to the days when he is cooking. Here is his lentil soup recipe.

Directions
Lightly brown onions in bacon drippings in a soup pot over medium low heat. Chop celery and carrots in a blender with a little water and add to onions. Add remaining ingredients. Bring to a boil over high heat, reduce heat to medium low and simmer for one-and-a-half hours.

Serves 10

Ingredients

2 qts. water
2 qts. beef broth
3 stalks celery
3 carrots
salt and pepper to taste
2 potatoes, diced
2 medium onions, chopped fine
4 Italian sausages, cooked, chopped medium
6 oz. tomato paste
2 bay leaves
3 TBS. bacon drippings
1 lb. lentils
3 cloves garlic, chopped fine

Joe Guzzetta was part of the crew that made the Normandy voyage in 1994. Here, the O'Brien *is outbound from San Francisco at the beginning of the trip. Photo: Ian Boyle.*

Kangaroo Tail Soup

ABOARD S.S. AMERICA
Captain HAROLD MILDE
Commander, U.S.N.R., Ret.

•

Clocks will be RETARDED One (1) Hour Tonight

Ingredients

2 lbs. onion, chopped fine
2 lbs. kangaroo meat,
  chopped in 1-inch dice
¼ C. vegetable oil
24 oz. stout, ale or beer
  (stout is preferred)
32 oz. beef stock
2 tsp. dried tarragon
salt and pepper to taste

One of our raffle prize dinners was based on a menu from the liner SS *America* which on August 10, 1955 offered Kangaroo Tail Soup as one of the courses. The 2000 Summer Olympics were going on in Sydney at the time so it seemed like a perfect "fit." The problem was where in the San Francisco Bay Area does one find kangaroo tail meat, or any other kind of kangaroo meat for that matter. My indispensable right hand in all these cooking endeavors, Aldred Chipman, a passionate cook himself, came through with flying colors. Not only did he find kangaroo meat at Molly Stone's Market in Sausalito (we weren't the only ones acknowledging the Olympics), but he developed this superb recipe.

Directions

Brown onions slowly in half the oil in a medium frying pan over medium low heat. Brown the meat in half the oil in a moderate-sized soup kettle over medium heat. When both are browned, add the onions to the meat. Add remaining ingredients. Simmer over medium low heat for approximately two hours or until the meat is tender.

Aldred Chipman tending to his now-famous kangaroo tail soup. Photo: S. Rose.

Serves 8

Mulligatawny Soup

Many tasty recipes originated in India, were refined by the British before the sun set on their empire, and came to America in the 1800s. One such dish is mulligatawny soup. We served this as part of the menu for one of our early raffle prize dinners based on a Pacific Coast Steamship Company menu of 1901. Unfortunately, the name of the ship was missing. Apparently the menu was standard issue for all that company's ships. Nonetheless, it shows that mulligatawny soup was a favorite dish, even at the beginning of the twentieth century. The word "mulligatawny" comes from an Indian word in the Tamil dialect meaning "pepper water." Don't let that throw you. It's a good spicy soup, but not nearly as hot as one might assume.

Directions

Brown the chicken in the butter in a soup kettle over medium heat, turning the pieces constantly to brown on all sides. Add carrot, pepper and apples. Cook for five minutes or until the vegetables are browned, stirring constantly from the bottom of the kettle. Sprinkle with the flour and curry powder and stir well. Add chicken stock, sugar,

Ingredients

3-lb. chicken, cut in eight
  pieces
¼ C. butter
¼ C. chopped carrots
¼ C. chopped green bell
  pepper
2 green apples (Granny
  Smith), chopped medium
1 TBS. flour
1 TBS. curry powder
4 qt. chicken stock
1 TBS. sugar
1 TBS. salt
1 tsp. parsley, chopped fine
2 whole cloves
pinch black pepper
pinch mace
1 C. tomato sauce

NOTES:
1. **To put a little zing in the soup, use Anaheim peppers instead of green bell peppers.**
2. **After removing the chicken, if you wish, you can purée the vegetables in a blender. Personally, I think the soup has a little more character if not puréed.**

The Jeremiah O'Brien's *overhead spice rack. Spices and seasonings are key ingredients in the international recipes we frequently recreate. Photo: S. Rose.*

salt, parsley, cloves, pepper and mace. Cook over low heat until chicken is tender, about forty-five minutes. Add tomato sauce and cook fifteen minutes longer. Remove the chicken, cut into small chunks. Return the chicken to the kettle, heat well and adjust seasonings. Serve hot with fluffy boiled rice if desired.

Serves 8.

PACIFIC COAST STEAMSHIP COMPANY

DINNER

BLUE POINTS

QUEEN OLIVES   CELERY   MIXED PICKLES

MULLAGATAWNY   CONSOMME IMPERIAL

BOILED FRESH FISH, HOLLANDAISE SAUCE

POTATOES AU NATURAL

VEAL, CELERY SAUCE

CHICKEN CROQUETTES, CREAM SAUCE   PEACH FRITTERS

PRIME RIBS OF BEEF AU JUS

LEG OF MUTTON WITH JELLY

HAM, CHAMPAGNE SAUCE

LETTUCE SALAD MAYONNAISE

CAULIFLOWER   RICE   STEWED TOMATOES

ENGLISH PLUM PUDDING, HARD AND BRANDY SAUCE

ASSORTED PASTRY AND PIES   PISTACHE ICE CREAM

NUTS   FRUITS IN SEASON   RAISINS

AMERICAN, EDAM AND SWISS CHEESE

TEA   COFFEE   CHOCOLATE

Any inattention or incivility on the part of an employee of the Steward's department should be immediately reported to the Purser. All complaints about the service in the dining room or in staterooms should be reported to the Chief Steward.

F 6-1 1. 10.23.1909, 5M

Minestrone

Before World War II there were two passenger liners that ran an overnight service between San Francisco and Los Angeles — the *Harvard* and the *Yale*. They belonged to the Los Angeles Steamship Company and were well-known at the time for their speed, service and food. We recreated the July 23, 1935 menu from the *Yale* for one of our raffle prize dinners aboard the *Jeremiah O'Brien*. From that menu comes this recipe for the classic Italian Minestrone. It's a great soup, almost a meal in itself. The key is fresh ingredients.

Directions

Bring the stock to a boil in a large kettle. Add remaining ingredients except for the cheese. Bring to a boil again, reduce heat and simmer the soup gently until the vegetables are tender and most of the stock is absorbed (about an hour). Stir in the Parmesan cheese. Serve. The soup should be thick enough that a wooden spoon will stand upright in it.

It works! Our spoon stuck up like a ship's mast when we tried this.

Serves 8.

Ingredients

1½ qt. beef stock
½ lb. salt pork, cut in 1-inch pieces
½ lb. fresh peas
½ lb. kidney beans (O.K. you can use canned here)
1 small green cabbage, shredded
½ lb. spinach, thoroughly rinsed
4 carrots, chopped
2 celery stalks, chopped
2 garlic cloves, finely minced (four or six is even better)
2 vine-ripened tomatoes, chopped
¼ C. raw rice
1 TBS. chopped parsley
½ tsp. fresh sage
3/4 C. Parmesan cheese
salt
pepper

NOTE:
For more color substitute a red cabbage for the green above.

Portuguese Turnip Soup (Sopa de Nabus)

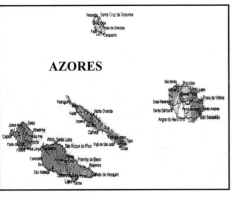

AZORES

Northern California, in the area around San Francisco, was settled by diverse cultures. The Chinese, Italian and Scandinavian peoples and traditions are well-known. But, with a little searching, one finds Japanese, Czech, Portuguese, Spanish, Greek, Samoan, Hawaiian, Philippine and many other types of cuisine in rich abundance. Rich Vannucci, of the *O'Brien*'s galley crew, is finely tuned to these various cooking styles. This recipe comes from the Portuguese of the San Joaquin Valley, most of whom are dairy farmers from the Azores.

Ingredients

1 gal. water
1 TBS. salt
1 large onion, chopped
4 cloves garlic, finely
   chopped
1½ lb. soup bones or short
   ribs with bones in
4 bunches turnip greens,
   chopped
4 large turnips, cubed
2 large potatoes, cubed
3 TBS. corn meal
2 TBS. fresh mint, coarsely
   chopped

Directions

In a large covered soup kettle, bring water, salt, onion, garlic and bones to a boil over high heat. Reduce heat to low and simmer two hours. Add turnip greens, turnips, potatoes and bring to a boil over medium heat. Reduce heat to low and simmer thirty minutes. Add corn meal and mint. Cook an additional ten minutes.

Serves 8.

NOTES:
1. Salt and pepper may be added to taste.
2. Rice, barley or pasta make a nice variation.
3. This soup is better the next day.
4. One link of finely chopped linguica, added while simmering, improves the richness.

Shrimp Gumbo

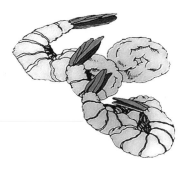

This is a classic dish from New Orleans and the lower Mississippi but famous throughout the world. It takes a bit of effort, but is well worth the time involved. We served it as the soup course in our "Showboat" menu, but it can be ladled over rice as an entree or even offered in small quantities as an appetizer for a Cajun- or Louisiana-style dinner. Also, you get a bonus meal from this. The chicken and sausage can be served later as a separate meal.

Directions

Heat the oil in a large (7 to 8 qt.) kettle over high heat. Brown the chicken parts in the hot oil, turning several times to brown evenly. Remove chicken to a heated platter and place, covered, in a 175°F. oven to keep it warm. Make the roux by gradually adding the flour to the oil in the kettle, stirring constantly. Cook over low heat until the color of milk chocolate (about forty-five minutes). Add the sausage, onion, green pepper, scallion tops, parsley and garlic. Cook over low heat stirring constantly for ten minutes. Add ¼ C. of water, the chicken and all the seasonings except the filé powder. Mix gently but thoroughly.

Ingredients

Gumbo Base
1 lb. smoked sausage (Polish, garlic, etc.) sliced in ¼ in. pieces
2 C. chopped onion
2/3 C. chopped green peppers
½ C. thinly sliced scallion tops
2 TBS. minced parsley
1 TBS. minced garlic
1 frying chicken, about 3 lb., cut in pieces
2 lb. whole fresh shrimp, peeled

Roux
2/3 C. vegetable oil
2/3 C. flour

Liquid and seasonings
2 qt. cold water
3 tsp. salt
1¼ tsp. freshly ground black pepper
1/8 tsp. cayenne
1 tsp. dried thyme
3 whole bay leaves, crushed
3 TBS. filé powder

NOTES:
1. **The key to good gumbo is to get the roux to the dark brown stage. This gives it a distinctive smoky flavor.**
2. **Filé is ground sassafras leaves and is one of the ingredients that gives this dish so many unusual and delicious flavors.**
3. **Gumbo is one of those dishes that improves with age. It is better the second day.**

Gradually add the rest of the water and bring to a boil, stirring gently. When it boils, reduce the heat to low and simmer for about forty-five minutes or until the chicken is very tender.

Remove all the chicken and some of the sausage with a slotted spoon. Place in a bowl, cover with plastic wrap and refrigerate for another meal.

Add the shrimp to the gumbo and cook about five minutes more. Remove the kettle from the heat and let the simmer die down. Add the filé powder and stir. Let stand in the kettle for five minutes before serving.

Serves 8.

S. S. Yale

B. V. WHITE, U.S.N.R. COMMANDER

T. BERTELSEN, CHIEF OFFICER   T. K. McDONALD, CHIEF ENGINEER

F. C. LEE, PURSER

F. E. KINTON, CHIEF STEWARD   WM. D. CASEY, SECOND STEWARD

"SOUVENIR MENU" This menu may be taken with you as a memento of your trip, or if you wish to mail it to a friend, the Purser will furnish you with an envelope.

VERANDA CAFE BALLROOM - 8.30 p.m. to 11.30 p.m.

DANCE MUSIC AND ENTERTAINMENT
DIRECTED BY
DAVE WILLIS

Los Angeles Steamship Company.

The Harvard *and* Yale *were well-known steamers running an overnight service between San Francisco and Los Angeles between World Wars I and II. We've featured the* Yale *twice in our raffle prize dinners. Author's collection.*

Once you learn how to manage the stove it's fairly simple. The large kettle directly over the fire, left center, contains soup, coming to boil, the smaller pot, right center, is something simmering, while the foil-covered dish, far right, is already cooked and staying warm. Photo: Author.

Time Capsule

The Normandy Voyage

The galley crew practiced their cooking skills for weeks before departure. It was learn-as-you-go, but they soon turned out great meals. Once we sailed, there was the seagoing routine of scheduled meals and a twenty-four hour day to deal with, but they quickly adjusted.

By now, the cooks had mastered the intricacies of the coal-fired galley stove. Each meal seemed better than the last. Al Martino, chief cook: "It was a learning process. Some things I knew and some I didn't know. It became difficult but after awhile we worked through it and it seemed to work all right. Most important, make sure you keep it fired up. Don't let it die on you or else you have to start all over again. Get in there early in the morning. I get in there about ten to four. You have to take the ashes out, shovel in new coal, and then start the fire. As long as you have enough time it's OK. But if you get in there late, you're putting yourself under too much pressure."

Appointment in Normandy (1995)
Walter W. Jaffee

Sweet Soup

This unusual dish comes from the Norwegian windjammers of the 19th century. Its popularity is proven by the fact that it was still served on the steam schooners that plied the West Coast during the first half of the twentieth century. Since many of the ships were manned by crews of Norwegian extraction, it makes sense that they would bring the dish with them. A good friend, John Smith, who was one of the prime movers of the *Lane Victory* project, talked about having this soup when he served on steam schooners before World War II. He said it was the best soup he ever had.

Ingredients

4 C. water
½ C. barley
½ C. rice
¼ C. prunes
¼ C. raisins
¼ C. currants
½ tsp. cinnamon
¼ tsp. allspice
¼ tsp. ground cloves
salt

Directions

Place the water and all the ingredients in a large pot or soup kettle. Bring to a boil over high heat. Reduce heat to low and let simmer for approximately thirty minutes.

Serves 6.

Dampfer „BARBAROSSA", 4. Januar 1899.

Frühstück.

Bananen.   Mandarinen   Ananas.

Hafergrütze.   Maisgries

Frische Milch und Sahne.

Gelée.   Marmelade.   Ingwer.

Geb Seezunge, Rémouladen-Sauce.

Beefsteak.   Hamburger Steak.

Hammelcôtelettes

Fricadellen.

Gebackene Kalbsnieren.

Salz-Kartoffeln,   Brat-Kartoffeln
Spiral-Kartoffeln

Yorker Schinken und Speck

Verlorene Eier auf Toast.

Eier auf Wunsch.

Eierkuchen mit Tomaten

Rührei mit Spargel

Buchweizenkuchen

Kalt: Roastbeef.   Sülze.

Chester- & Edamer-Käse.

Brödchen   Kaffeebrod   Hörnchen.

Kaffee   Thee   Chocolade   Cacao

Breakfast.

Bananas   Mandarines   Pine-apples

Oatmeal.   Hominy.

Fresh milk and cream.

Jelly.   Marmalade.   Ginger.

Fried sole, rémoulade sauce.

Beefsteak.   Hamburg beefsteak.

Mutton chops.

Meat balls.

Fried calf's kidney.

Boiled potatoes.   Fried potatoes

Spiral potatoes.

Yorkshire ham and bacon.

Poached eggs on toast.

Eggs to order.

Omelet with tomatoes

Scrambled eggs with asparagus.

Buckwheat cakes.

Cold: Roastbeef.   Brawn.

Chester- & Dutch cheese.

Rolls.   Biscuits.

Coffee   Tea   Chocolate   Cocoa

This menu from the German liner Barbarossa *shows some of the fare offered on trans-Atlantic ships in the late 1880s. If this was breakfast, imagine what dinner was like!*

Salads

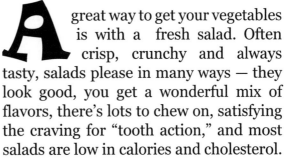

A great way to get your vegetables is with a fresh salad. Often crisp, crunchy and always tasty, salads please in many ways — they look good, you get a wonderful mix of flavors, there's lots to chew on, satisfying the craving for "tooth action," and most salads are low in calories and cholesterol.

Although usually served as a "preliminary" or side dish, a good salad can be a meal in itself. Seafood salads, chef's salad and cobb salad fall into this category. Of course, "Soup and a Salad" are always popular as a quick lunch.

We serve salad as a separate course when we recreate shipboard menus of the past. It makes the dinner seem more special. Starting with an appetizer, we then serve either a soup or a fish course followed by salad. Then comes the main course with accompanying vegetables and fresh-baked bread or rolls. Finally, we top it off with a couple of desserts. Sometimes three.

Included in the following are the traditional (tossed green) and the not so traditional (Solomongundy) salads. I've included the more popular recipes from our raffle prize dinners, rounded it out with a couple of others, but left out those found in most other cookbooks.

Asparagus Salad with Champagne Saffron Vinaigrette

One thing that's always surprising is just how gritty fresh asparagus can be. It must have to do with the way it's grown, but for something so lacking in creases and crevices in which to accumulate sand, it seems to have more than its fair share. Fresh, young asparagus has a distinctive and very pleasing flavor. This recipe is interesting because you don't often see this vegetable on its own as a salad. It was part of our *Titanic* menu.

Directions

Snap off and discard woody base of each asparagus stalk. Cook in a pot of boiling, salted water from three to five minutes, or until tender. Drain and run under cold water until completely cooled. Drain well.

Meanwhile, in a large bowl, stir saffron into 1 tsp. boiling water; let stand for two minutes until softened. Stir in champagne vinegar, mustard and sugar. Whisking, drizzle in olive oil. Season with salt and pepper to taste. Add asparagus and diced bell pepper, toss to coat. Arrange lettuce on plates, place asparagus on top.

Serves 6.

Ingredients

1 ½ lb. asparagus
¼ tsp. saffron
1 ½ TBS. champagne vinegar
1/2 tsp. Dijon mustard
1 pinch granulated sugar
3 TBS. extra virgin olive oil
salt and pepper
1/2 C. each, diced red and yellow bell pepper
Butter lettuce

NOTES:
1. When buying asparagus, select the smaller spears. The narrower the stalk, the better the flavor and the more tender it is.
2. Butter lettuce has a nice color and texture and works well as a bed for the asparagus. You might want to save some of the diced bell pepper and sprinkle it on top after the asparagus is in place.

R.M.S. "TITANIC."

APRIL 14, 1912.

HORS D'ŒUVRE VARIÈS
OYSTERS

COMSOMMÉ OLGA   CREAM OF BARLEY

SALMON, MOUSSELINE SAUCE, CUCUMBER

FILET MIGNONS LILI
SAUTÉ OF CHICKEN, LYONNAISE
VEGETABLE MARROW FARCIE

LAMB, MINT SAUCE
ROAST DUCKLING, APPLE SAUCE
SIRLOIN OF BEEF CHATEAU POTATOES

GREEN PEAS   CREAMED CARROTS
BOILED RICE
PARMENTIER & BOILED NEW POTATOES

PUNCH ROMAINE

ROAST SQUAB & CRESS
COLD ASPARAGUS VINAIGRETTE
PÂTE DE FOIE GRAS
CELERY

WALDORF PUDDING
PEACHES IN CHARTREUSE JELLY
CHOCOLATE & VANILLA ECLAIRS
FRENCH ICE CREAM

One would guess the Titanic *was trying to achieve "understated elegance" with this menu, but the effect is quite ordinary.*

Butter Bean Salad

I suspect there's a good reason that Italian cuisine is so popular. Rich Vannucci often calls on his Italian heritage when cooking for the ship's crew on the *O'Brien*. Here's another example of his excellent cooking style. He says the recipe is native to Liguria, Italy which is the region surrounding Genoa, a famous seaport (Columbus set out from here).

Directions

Drain beans. Chill all ingredients. Combine in a large salad bowl. Mix dressing and add to salad. Toss.

Serves 8

Ingredients

2 C. cooked butter beans
1 C. celery, finely chopped
6 green onions, chopped
2 hard cooked eggs, sliced
8 tsp. chopped pimento
8 tsp. fresh sweet basil, chopped
1 TBS. black pepper
4 TBS. green pepper, chopped
4 cloves garlic, finely chopped
4 anchovy fillets, very finely chopped

Dressing

¼ C. 70 grain vinegar (4 Monks) or lemon juice
¼ C. olive oil

Christopher Columbus, born in Genoa in 1451.

Jimmy Farras removing fresh bread from the oven. Photo: George Bonawit.

Jimmy Farras was trained at the California Culinary Academy and signed on as third cook for the Normandy voyage. The stove was a challenge to him.

Time Capsule

The Normandy Voyage

"That took a little while, to get used to the baking. There were different hot spots you had to rotate. A lot of pastries, sometimes cakes would be cooked on one side and raw on the other so you'd have to spin the cakes or pies. And you did a lot of the baking in the morning because when you baked, you couldn't fry on top of the stove because it was too cool. On a coal burner, it's not like you can leave it. On an electric stove, you turn the thermostat on and you walk away. Here you had to keep shoveling the coal for the next meal, to stack it so it would stay hot. There were no thermostats so you had to basically go by feel. Like if you were deep-frying breaded prawns, if they're browning within two minutes it's too hot, so you'd put them [the frying pans] up on [inverted] pie tins to cool down. Things like that you got used to. That was a pretty big highlight for me, being in the galley like that and that coal-burning stove."

Appointment in Normandy (1995)
Walter W. Jaffee

Caesar Salad

Colanders, mixing bowls, baking pans, pots, you-name-it — all supersized; the Jeremiah O'Brien *has enough utensils for every occasion, even Caesar salad. Photo: S. Rose.*

The best Caesar Salad I ever had was years ago at the Empress Hotel in Victoria, Canada. Our waiter started with a wooden bowl, a sprinkle of salt and a large clove of garlic. He worked a metal spoon around and around the bowl, mashing the garlic against the sides and bottom. After a short time he showed us the bowl and the garlic had vanished! It was like a magic trick. Next, he put in four anchovy fillets, went to work with his spoon and they vanished, too. He continued with the rest of the salad, but that bit of legerdemain with the garlic and anchovies has stayed with me to this day. I've tried to do the same thing, but always end up with little bits of garlic and anchovy around the inside of the bowl. Maybe in another twenty years or so I'll master the trick. Anyway, this is absolutely the best salad you could possibly make.

Directions

Put a dash of salt in a wooden salad bowl. With a tablespoon, mash the garlic in the bowl, spreading it around the sides and bottom as much as possible. Do the same with the anchovies. Meanwhile, place an egg in a small pot, cover with

Ingredients

1 head romaine lettuce, rinsed and dried, torn into bite-sized pieces
1 large clove garlic
6 anchovy fillets
1 egg
½ C. grated parmesan cheese
2 C. garlic croutons
salt

Dressing

¼ C. olive oil
1 TBS. rice wine vinegar
1 TBS. Dijon mustard
2 tsp. Worcestershire sauce
1 tsp. lemon juice
dash ground white pepper
dash ground allspice

We don't have any wooden bowls on the *Jeremiah O'Brien*, so we do this with metal bowls. Instead of mashing the garlic and anchovies, we mince them and mix them in with the dressing. The wooden bowl method distributes the flavors more evenly, making for a more enjoyable salad.

water and put on high heat. As soon as the water comes to a rolling boil, remove egg and put under cold water. Place the lettuce into the bowl. Break egg and scoop out onto the lettuce. Put all of the dressing ingredients in a small bowl, mixing thoroughly with a fork to emulsify the oil. Pour over salad. Add the cheese and the croutons. Toss and serve.

Serves 4-6.

Bev Masterson, right, preparing the officers' saloon for a raffle prize dinner for eight. Below, the Jeremiah O'Brien *at Pier 32, where she sometimes berths when not at Fisherman's Wharf. Right photo: S. Rose, below, Marvin Jensen.*

Solomongundy

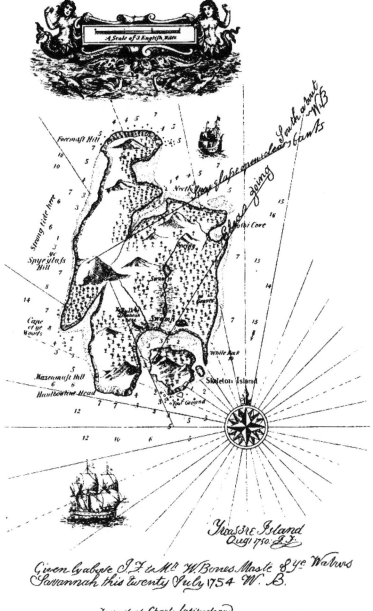

Bartholomew Roberts

This is another dish we prepared for the "Patrick O'Brian Dinner." It is basically a chef's salad. The name dates from 1730 where we find the Englishman Charles Carter referring to a ragout of half-roasted game as "Salad Mogundy." One source on pirate fare refers to "Solomon Grundy" or "salamagundi" as a sort of spicy chef's salad that included whatever was handy: "Bits of meat, fish, turtle and shellfish were marinated in a mixture of herbs, palm hearts, garlic, spiced wine and oil, and then served with hard-boiled eggs and pickled onions, cabbage, grapes and olives."

A second pirate book refers to "salmagundi/salmagundy" as: "Meat of any kind — including turtle, duck or pigeon — was roasted, chopped into chunks and marinated in spiced wine. Imported salted meat, herring and anchovies also were added. When ready to serve, the smoked and salted meats were combined with hard-boiled eggs and whatever fresh or pickled vegetables were available, including palm hearts, cabbage, mangoes, onions and olives. The result was tossed together with oil, vinegar, garlic, salt, pepper, mustard seed and other seasonings."

and other seasonings."

The pirate Bartholomew Roberts was eating salmagundi for breakfast when he was surprised by British warships off West Africa in 1722.

In time solomongundy has come to mean miscellany, hodgepodge, olio or any other thing you want it to mean. I once saw solomongundy listed on a menu in Nova Scotia, ordered it, and was served pickled herring on lettuce. My hopes were for something more exotic, but one man's solomongundy is another man's pickled herring.

Directions

Line a large serving dish with the lettuce. Chop the egg yolks and egg whites separately. Arrange the meats, vegetables, anchovies, yolks, whites and herbs in pleasing and fanciful groupings.

Combine the oil, vinegar, lemon juice, mustard and salt and pepper to taste and mix vigorously. Pour this dressing over the solomongundy. Garnish with nasturtiums. Serves 6-8.

This is a fairly simple and tasty salad. In the spirit of the original solomongundy we substituted smoked turkey breast for the chicken, snow peas for the snap peas. The nasturtium flowers are edible and add a little extra zing and color.

Ingredients

1 head romaine or other leaf lettuce, broken in pieces.
8 hard-boiled eggs
1 lb. boneless breast of chicken, cooked, cut in thin strips
1 lb. smoked ham, cut in thin strips
2 cucumbers, peeled and thinly sliced.
3 ribs of celery, thinly sliced
3 shallots, peeled and thinly sliced
2 TBS. nonpareil capers
2 TBS. chopped fresh parsley
½ lb. snap peas or French beans, blanched
1 2-oz. can anchovies.

Dressing

6 TBS. olive oil
1 TBS. vinegar
1 TBS. lemon juice
½ tsp. dry mustard
salt and pepper
nasturtiums

NOTE:
You can be creative with this dish, substituting or adding as you like. The dressing might not look like enough when you first put it on, but it mixes well and is just right.

NATIONAL LIBERTY SHIP MEMORIAL

~ SS JEREMIAH O'BRIEN ~

MENU
Friday, June 26, 1998

Swordfish Fritters

Solomongundy

Bisque de Homard

*Roast Pork, Sage & Onion Stuffing
Onion Gravy*

Yellow Rice
Short French Bastards

Shrewsbury Cakes
Spotted Dog *with Custard Sauce*

Wines ~ Coffee

Based on the Aubrey-Maturin novels of Patrick O'Brien
Dinner aboard HMS *Surprise*, late 1700s

Our guests for the Patrick O'Brian dinner were presented with this menu. By the way, you'll find the recipe for Spotted Dog in the dessert section.

Syrian Salad

Some of the best cooking in the world comes from Syria. I fondly remember a lamb dish called *kibbee* that a Syrian neighbor made when I was a boy. Here, Rich Vannucci gives us a terrific salad that comes from that middle eastern country.

Directions

Boil beans in liberally salted water until done but not soft. Set aside to cool. When beans are room temperature, mix all the ingredients, except the parsley, in a large salad bowl. Mix in the parsley. Cool the salad in the refrigerator for three hours before serving.

Serves 8.

Ingredients

1 lb. great northern beans
1 bunch fresh cilantro, chopped medium
1 red bell pepper, chopped medium
1 green bell pepper, chopped medium
1 bunch green onion or 1 red onion, chopped medium
1 C. olive oil
1 C. fresh lemon juice
1 TBS. cider vinegar
1 bunch parsley, chopped fine
salt and pepper to taste
dash of sage

Note:
This salad can stay in the refrigerator for up to a week and still taste great. As a variation, pine nuts may be added to the mix.

The entire crew pitches in for a raffle prize dinner: Wes Masterson, foreground, chops vegetables, while behind him Aldred Chipman checks his bread dough and behind him the author (almost invisible) works on the entree. Photo: S. Rose.

Ingredients

For the Salad:
2 lbs. new potatoes
1 head red-leaf or green
  leaf lettuce
¼ lb. mushrooms
1 C. sliced fresh toma-
  toes (vine-ripened)

Dressing

3 TBS. olive oil
1 TBS. rice wine vinegar
1 TBS. Dijon mustard
1 TBS. honey

VARIATIONS: **Any one of these or in combination, according to your taste.**
1. Add 1 or 2 sliced hard-cooked eggs or half a dozen sliced salted hard-cooked quail eggs.
2. Add about four forkfulls of Japanese pickled ginger.
3. Add 1 clove finely chopped garlic.
4. Substitute garlic flavored walnut oil for olive oil.
5. Delete the tomatoes.
6. Delete the mushrooms.
7. Add 1 thinly sliced green onion.
8. Add 1 sliced cucumber and 1 TBS. fresh dill.
9. Add ¼ C. sunflower seeds.
10. Add ¼ C. toasted chopped walnuts.

The Incredible Salad

This salad came about when we had a weekend guest and in a fit of inspiration I whipped together a salad for dinner. At the first bite, our guest said, "This tastes incredible," and that became the name of the salad. She liked it so much she hardly ate anything else at that meal.

Directions

If potatoes are larger than walnut size, cut in halves or quarters. Place potatoes in pot, cover with water, add dash of salt, turn heat to high until boiling, then reduce to medium. Cook about 1/2 hour or until knife point goes easily into potato. Remove from heat, replace hot water with cold, let cool to room temperature. (You can hurry this up by just letting the cold water run over the potatoes in the pot for 15 minutes or so). Tear lettuce into bite sized pieces, place in bowl. Slice tomatoes, potatoes and mushrooms, add to lettuce. Mix dressing, pour over salad and toss.

Serves 4.

Tossed Green Salad with Honey-Mustard Dressing

Ingredients

1 head romaine lettuce

Dressing
¼ C. extra virgin olive oil
1 TBS. Dijon mustard
1 TBS. honey
1 tsp. rice wine vinegar
salt
pepper

Quite often we'll use this basic salad as a "fill-in" on one of our ship's menus. Usually it's when there are a lot of other courses in the menu that require a lot of time in preparation. This salad can be mixed, tossed and served in almost as little time as it takes to describe it. And it's always a hit. The secret is the dressing.

Directions

Wash lettuce in cold water and dry thoroughly. Tear into bite-sized pieces.

Mix the ingredients for the dressing so they are well-combined. Pour over the salad, season to taste with salt and pepper and toss.

Serves 8.

VARIATIONS:
1. **Try other types of lettuce. Mix two or three (but not iceberg; the texture is wrong) with the romaine.**
2. **Add a peeled, sliced cucumber.**
3. **Add a couple of thinly sliced tomatoes. (Be sure they are vine-ripened! Most super-market tomatoes are tasteless and you might as well add a cup of sawdust as use one of them).**
4. **Add two thinly sliced green onions.**
5. **Try a sprig of dill weed, chopped.**

NOTE:
The secret here is to use rice wine vinegar. The flavor is less overpowering and complements the mustard and honey nicely.

Tossed Pear Salad with Devil Nuts

Ingredients

1 head red leaf or butter lettuce
1 ripe pear, diced
3 TBS. extra virgin olive oil
4 oz. gorgonzola cheese, crumbled
1 tsp. rice wine vinegar
salt
pepper

For the nuts
1 lb. pecans, almonds, walnuts or mix
1 tsp. salt
1 tsp. black pepper
1 tsp. chipotle powder
1 tsp. sweet paprika
1 TBS. butter
½ C. maple syrup

NOTE:
English Stilton or Maytag Bleu cheese may be substituted for the gorgonzola.

Aldred Chipman contributed this recipe after serving it at several potluck dinners on the *O'Brien* to great enthusiasm and overwhelming cries for "more." The key ingredient is the "devil nuts."

Directions
For the nuts

Combine spices, butter and syrup in a non-stick saucepan and heat until the butter is melted. Add the nuts and cook over medium heat until the syrup is reduced by about one-half. Place the nuts in a single layer on a non-stick cookie sheet. Bake in a 325°F. oven for 18-25 minutes.

For the Salad

Wash and dry lettuce, tear into bite-sized pieces and place in salad bowl. Add pear, oil, vinegar, salt, pepper and nuts. Toss.

Serves 4.

Warm Potato-Celery Root-Apple Salad

Our inspiration for this was a menu from the steamer *Acapulco* dated 1875. Recreating that menu took a bit of research because many of the items listed aren't found in modern cookbooks. This salad was a mixture of two or three recipes, a bit of luck and a benevolent cooking god looking over our shoulders. It came out far better than we had any right to expect.

Directions

Boil the whole potatoes thirty minutes or until cooked. Remove from heat, pour off water, add cold water to fill pot and let cool for five minutes.

Boil the eggs for ten minutes. Peel and slice.

Meanwhile, melt 1 TBS. butter in a medium pot. Add the celery root and cook five minutes. Cover with broth and simmer fifteen minutes. In a separate pan, melt the remaining butter, stir in the flour and add to the celery root to thicken.

Mix the dressing and set aside to let the flavors meld.

Dice the apples, put in a mixing bowl with the lettuce. Add celery root and sauce, eggs, potatoes, dressing and toss.

Serves 8.

Ingredients

For the salad

4 medium new potatoes
2 TBS. butter
1 TBS. flour
1 celery root, peeled and diced
8 oz. beef broth
2 eggs
2 C. butter lettuce
2 Red Delicious apples
2 tsp. dry dill weed
salt, pepper

Dressing

¼ C. olive oil
2 tsp. rice wine vinegar
1 TBS. Dijon mustard
1 TBS. mayonnaise
1 garlic clove, minced

Celery root, also called celeriac, is a fun vegetable. The taste is similar to celery, but much milder. Sometimes it's served as a side dish.

Warm Salmon Salad

This is a good cold weather salad, when you want something to warm your insides. It's low in calories, yet has a surprisingly pleasant combination of flavors that will have your guests clamoring for the recipe.

Directions

In a small roasting pan, coat both sides of the salmon steak with the olive oil. Sprinkle with the chopped garlic and salt and pepper. Place about six inches under a broiler and cook for fifteen minutes, turning once at the halfway point.

Meanwhile, rinse and dry lettuce, tear into bite-sized pieces. Put lettuce in salad bowl.

Remove bones and skin from cooked salmon, break fish into small pieces and add to lettuce. Mix dressing, add to salad and toss.

Serves 2 as a main course or 4-6 as a side dish.

Ingredients

6-8 oz. salmon steak
1 head red-leaf lettuce
2 cloves garlic, chopped
   medium
1 TBS. olive oil
salt
pepper
grated Parmesan
   cheese

Dressing

2 TBS. olive oil
1 tsp. rice wine vinegar
2 tsp. Dijon mustard
1 tsp. lemon juice

NOTE:
Be sure to get all the chopped garlic out of the roasting pan and include it in the salad. It adds an extra dimension of flavor.

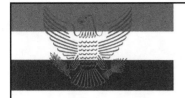

S. S. AMERICA

HORS D'OEUVRES - VORSPEISEN
Smoked Salmon or Eel

Matjes Herring in Cream

Antipasto Italienne   Salmon Salad

Chilled Orange Juice

Gabelbissen in Wine

BUFFET, GOURMET - KALTES BÜFFET
Passengers are cordially invited to view and make their selection

SOUPS - SUPPEN

Potage Jeannette

Clam Broth with Celery

FISH - FISCH
Fried Fresh Plaice, Remoulade, Cole Slaw (Goldbutt)
Poached Fresh Salmon, Hollandaise Sauce, Parsley Potatoes (Lachs)

EGGS - EIER

Shirred Eggs sur le Plat

Omelette a la Suisse or Plain

ENTREES - ZWISCHEN-GERICHT
Boiled Kasseler Ribs, Green Kale, Bermuda Potatoes
Assorted Vegetable Lunch with Poached Egg (Gemüse Platte mit Eier)
Supreme of Turkey a la King on Toast (Truthahn Frikasse)
Hot Roast Beef Sandwich Garni, French Fried Potatoes
From the Grill: Broiled Calves Sweetbreads on Toast

COMPOTES - KOMPOTT
Peaches, Cherries or Mixed

VEGETABLES - GEMÜSE
Braised White Cabbage

Puree of Peas   Lima Beans   Shell Macaroni au Parmesan

POTATOES - KARTOFFELN
Boiled, Mashed or au Gratin (Gekochter, Püree oder au Gratin)

COLD DISHES - KALTER AUFSCHNITT
Assorted Delicatess Plate, Garni (Gemischter Kalter Aufschnitt, Garniert)
Various Kinds of Fresh and Smoked Sausages
(Verschiedene Frische und Geräucherte Wurst)

SALADS - SALATE
Heart of Lettuce   Sliced Tomato   Pickled Beets   Cole Slaw
Dressings: French, Lemon or Nanking

DESSERTS - SÜSS-SPEISEN

Boston Cream Pie   Apricot Sherbet   Rice Custard Pudding

Assorted Cookies   Strawberry Jello

Raspberry Ice Cream, Nabisco Wafers

CHEESE - KÄSE
Young American, Old Hampshire or Harzer Cheese with Toasted Crackers

---

White or Rye Bread   Pumpernickel   Ry-Krisp

Fresh Fruit in Season (Frisches Obst)

Coffee   Tea   Fresh Milk

Kaffee   Tee   Frische Milch

WB-CCL-5   **Thursday, August 11, 1955**

UNITED STATES LINES

Because she was on the Germany-New York run, the SS America*'s menu headings were listed in both languages. Author's collection.*

A number of our seafood dishes (as well as other courses in the raffle prize dinners) were inspired by menus from American President Lines' passenger ships. Top, SS President Cleveland *on one of her six-week cruises to the Far East sometime in the 1960s; above,* SS President Wilson *and* SS President Cleveland *passing along the San Francisco waterfront; left, APL menu cover. Photos: Top and above, American President Lines; left, author's collection.*

Seafood

Seafarers and seafood are a natural combination. But seafarer or landlubber, it would be hard to find anyone that doesn't like seafood. Of course, the fresher, the better — a breakfast of flying fish harvested from the deck of a heavily loaded freighter in the early morning, crab and rock lobster trapped while laying at anchor waiting for a berth, even shark, caught with hook and line. A mariner and his fish — live or cooked — are seldom far apart.

Following are some good and unusual recipes from the raffle prize dinners, from the *O'Brien* galley crew and a couple of others thrown in for variety.

First class dining was in the California Room, right. The President Cleveland *and* President Wilson *were sister ships (the two ships were so similar that this photo can't be identified as to which ship). Top, the passenger list named ship's senior officers and first class passengers. Above, the APL price list for alcoholic beverages. Photos: right, American President Lines, top and above, author's collection.*

Baked Salmon Fillet

Salmon can almost stand alone as a top-notch dish. A little oil, salt and pepper and you've got a great meal. But in this recipe Joe Guzzetta adds a few Italian touches that really bring out the flavor and make this dish outstanding.

Ingredients

2½-3 lb. salmon fillet
1 TBS. olive oil
1 TBS. butter, melted
2 oz. white wine
2 cloves garlic, chopped fine
2 oz. lemon juice
parsley, chopped

Directions

Brush baking pan with olive oil and butter. Blend wine, garlic and lemon juice and brush on salmon. Place salmon on baking pan. Be sure to fold the tail end under so the fillet is the same thickness across. Bake in a pre-heated 400°F. oven for ten minutes. Test for doneness. Sprinkle with parsley.

Serves 8

Joe Guzzetta in the galley during a steaming weekend. Photo: Author.

Cioppino

Ingredients

1 large striped bass,
   rock cod or other
   white-fleshed fish, cut
   in pieces
1 Dungeness crab,
   steamed and cut in
   pieces
1 Maine lobster,
   steamed and cut in
   pieces
1 lb. mussels
1 dozen clams
1 C. shelled shrimp
½ C. olive oil
3 TBS. chopped parsley
2 finely chopped cloves
   garlic
1 large bell pepper,
   chopped
1 large onion, coarsely
   chopped
1 C. sliced mushrooms
1 C. chopped tomatoes
2 whole cloves
3 bay leaves
1 C. red wine
salt
cayenne

NOTES
1. Leave the shells on
both the crab and
lobster for added flavor
while cooking. Remove
them before serving.
2. You can leave out the
clams and mussels and
still have a fantastic
dish.

This is the West Coast answer to the classic French bouillabaisse or American fish stew. Most people agree it originated with the Italian fishing families of San Francisco, although those of Portuguese extraction in other parts of California claim it as original. In any case, Cioppino has become a classic San Francisco dish. The key ingredient is Dungeness crab, a Bay Area favorite. The addition of Maine lobster gives it an extra dimension, although you can certainly leave it out.

Directions

Heat olive oil over medium heat in a large iron pot (or soup kettle). Add parsley, garlic, pepper, onion and mushrooms and cook for about five minutes or until the onion is softened. Mix in the tomatoes, cloves, bay leaves and wine. Cover and simmer for one hour. Season to taste with salt and cayenne. Add the fish and cook for about twenty minutes without stirring. Add the shrimp, mussels, clams, lobster and crab and simmer about five minutes. Serve in bowls and accompany with plenty of crusty Italian bread (to soak up the soup) and chianti.

Serves 8.

Colorado Mountain Trout Sauté with Toasted Almond Butter

Our raffle prize dinners on the *Jeremiah O'Brien* have two unique features: they are cooked on a coal-fired stove and the menu for each dinner is based on a shipboard menu of the past. In this case, we did a menu from the passenger liner SS *President Roosevelt*, which American President Lines operated in its around-the-world service from just after World War II until the late 1960s. The interesting thing about many menus (in restaurants as well as on board passenger liners) is the way they are dressed up to make everything sound unusual or interesting. In this one the trout was presumably caught in the mountains of Colorado (probably at a fish farm). It was then fried, but sauté sounds so much classier. Then some butter was melted and almonds toasted in it, thus we get "Colorado Mountain Trout Sauté with Toasted Almond Butter." This is basically Almond Trout or "Trout Amandine." By whatever name it's good as a main course or as a fish dish before the main course.

Directions

Season trout with salt and pepper. Dip in milk, then dredge in flour. Heat vegetable oil at medium high in skillet to

Ingredients

6 trout, cleaned and filleted
salt
pepper
milk for dipping
flour for dredging
vegetable oil

Toasted Almond Butter

¼ C. butter
½ C. blanched, slivered
   almonds
fresh sage for garnish
thin sliced lemon for garnish

NOTES:
1. If you're serving this as a fish course before the entrée, cut each fish in half, lengthwise, and serve one fillet per person.
2. When you toast the almonds, watch them closely. They will turn color before your eyes. Cooked too long, they turn black and bitter.
3. Parsley works just as well as sage, but I get so darned tired of seeing parsley on everything, it's a pleasant change to use something else.

a depth of ¼ inch. Sauté the trout until they are golden brown on both sides (about 2 minutes per side). Remove from pan. Drain the oil from the pan and add the butter. Sauté the almonds in the butter until they are brown. Pour the butter and almonds over the trout. Garnish each plate with a slice or two of lemon and a few leaves of sage.

Serves 6 as a main course or 12 as a fish course.

Lake trout.

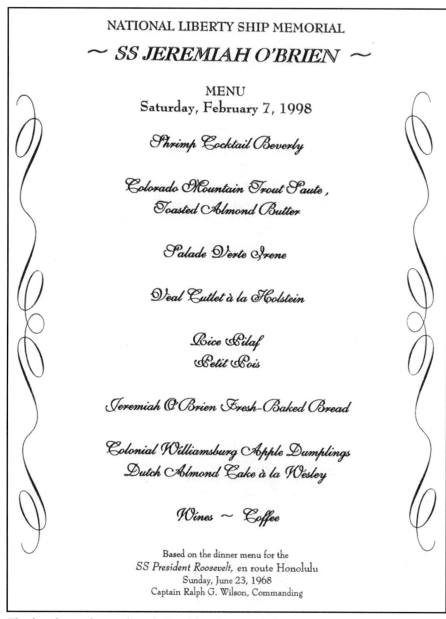

NATIONAL LIBERTY SHIP MEMORIAL

~ SS JEREMIAH O'BRIEN ~

MENU
Saturday, February 7, 1998

Shrimp Cocktail Beverly

Colorado Mountain Trout Saute,
Toasted Almond Butter

Salade Verte Irene

Veal Cutlet à la Holstein

Rice Pilaf
Petit Pois

Jeremiah O'Brien Fresh-Baked Bread

Colonial Williamsburg Apple Dumplings
Dutch Almond Cake à la Wesley

Wines ~ Coffee

Based on the dinner menu for the
SS President Roosevelt, en route Honolulu
Sunday, June 23, 1968
Captain Ralph G. Wilson, Commanding

The fine dining featured on the President Roosevelt *has inspired more than one of our raffle prize dinners.*

Time Capsule

Jeremiah O'Brien
The Man

DONT TREAD ON ME

Many people are curious as to just who Jeremiah O'Brien was. What did he do to get a ship named after him? It began at the outbreak of the Revolutionary War ...

By 1775, the long-festering problems between the American colonies and the British Crown had reached the breaking point. On June 2, 1775, the armed schooner Margaretta, *together with two sloops, entered the harbor in Machias, Maine to demand lumber for British troop barracks in Boston. The townspeople refused, erecting a Liberty Pole as a symbol of their defiance.*

Stealthily commandeering a British sloop and loading it with arms and ammunition, the colonists sailed downstream to capture the Margaretta. *Jeremiah O'Brien, a thirty-one-year-old lumberjack, was chosen captain. His crew of thirty-five had one loaf of bread, a few pieces of pork and a barrel of water. Their weaponry consisted of twenty shotguns with three rounds of ball and powder each, one small cannon, a few axes and swords and some thirty pitchforks.*

Coming within hailing distance of the British ship, O'Brien shouted, "In America's name, I demand you surrender." The British fired a volley that killed two men. The Americans answered with their one gun. As the ships crashed into each other, Capt. O'Brien lashed them together. Leading a select group of twenty pitchforkmen, he boarded the British vessel and continued the fight hand to hand. The British were no match for the colonists and soon Jeremiah O'Brien hauled down the British Ensign, winning the first naval battle of the Revolutionary War.

The sloop, renamed the Machias Liberty, *was the first American armed cruiser of the Revolution and, in a sense, the first true Liberty ship.*

The Last Liberty (1993)
Walter W. Jaffee

Crawfish Étouffée

The O'Brien's coal-fired stove and giant pots are just right to "smother" étouffée. Photo: S. Rose

Crawfish can be had at most large supermarkets. They might have to order it for you, but they can get it. Otherwise you could substitute shrimp and have a dish that tastes just as good. This is a standard in many New Orleans restaurants and a classic example of the cooking of that region. The term étouffée means "to smother" and is a reference to the long cooking time with the lid on before the crawfish are added. This was the fish course in our "Showboat" dinner but served over rice, it makes a good one-course meal.

Directions

In a large (5 to 6 qt.) pot, melt ½ C. of the butter over low heat. Gradually add the flour, stirring constantly until a medium brown roux (about the color of peanut butter) develops, about 20 minutes. Add onions, scallions, pepper, celery, basil and remaining butter. Sauté over medium heat for thirty minutes. Add remaining seasonings, tomato sauce, Worcestershire sauce, Tabasco sauce and chicken broth. Cook covered on low heat for one hour. At lowest heat setting, add crawfish, lemon juice and parsley. Cook for five minutes. Top each serving with two or three of the whole crawfish.

Serves 8.

Ingredients

1 C. butter
¼ C. flour
1 C. onion, chopped
1 C. scallions, chopped
¼ C. green pepper, chopped
½ C. celery, chopped
1 TBS. fresh basil, chopped, or ½ tsp. dried
1 tsp. salt
¼ C. tomato sauce
1 tsp. Worcestershire sauce
Tabasco to taste
2 C. chicken broth
2 lb. crawfish or shrimp, peeled
1 TBS. lemon juice
¼ C. minced parsley
Additional whole crawfish for garnish

Fish in a Bag

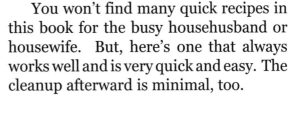

Ingredients

- *2 white fish fillets (catfish, cod, sole, trout, etc.)*
- *1 plastic bag, the kind the newspaper comes in on a rainy day (or a brown paper bag)*
- *1/4 C. flour*
- *1 TBS. paprika*
- *1 tsp. freshly ground black pepper*
- *½ tsp. salt*
- *1 clove garlic, chopped*
- *¼ C. extra virgin olive oil.*

You won't find many quick recipes in this book for the busy househusband or housewife. But, here's one that always works well and is very quick and easy. The cleanup afterward is minimal, too.

Directions

Pour the oil into a skillet at low heat. Add chopped garlic. Meanwhile, place flour and seasonings in plastic bag and, holding it closed, shake to mix. Rinse and dry fish fillets. Place fish fillets in bag, hold closed and shake to coat fish. Remove fillets to work surface. Throw away the bag and whatever's left inside it. Raise temperature on skillet to medium high. Remove garlic to serving plates. When oil is hot, add fish. Fry two to seven minutes on each side, depending on thickness, or until done. Place on serving plates with crunchy garlic pieces on top.

Serves 2.

Fried Catfish

Catfish are one of the most under-rated fish in today's cuisine. Thanks to fish farming, catfish are plentiful year round and found in almost every market. Of course, the best tasting ones are those right out of the river. But fresh store-bought will work almost as well. My first experience with fried catfish coated with cornmeal was at a "down home" restaurant called The Boondocks near Beaumont, Texas. There, the whole fish was deep-fried. Most homes don't have a fryer large enough, so I think this variation works just as well. It's a simple dish, relatively easy to prepare, but the sweet flavor of the fish mixed with the hot seasonings is outstanding.

Directions

Rinse the fish pieces under cold running water and dry thoroughly with paper towels. Put them in a bowl and add cold milk to cover. Combine the corn meal and seasonings in another bowl. Preheat the oil in a deep fryer to 375°F. (you can also use a skillet on the stove at medium-high). When the oil is hot, quickly lift the pieces of fish out of the milk (four or six at a time, then prepare

Ingredients

1 medium-sized to large
  freshwater catfish,
  cut crosswise into
  half-inch wide pieces
Cold milk for soaking
1½ C. yellow corn meal
2 ¼ tsp. salt
1 tsp. freshly ground
  black pepper
1½ tsp. cayenne
Vegetable oil for deep
  frying

NOTE:
You might find variations on this recipe that call for fish fillets. I prefer leaving the bones in. They add flavor and they give you something to hold on to with your fingers, which is the only proper way to eat this dish.

the next batch while the first is cooking), roll them in the seasoned meal. Lay them flat, not touching, on a work surface to dry for a few minutes. Fry until golden brown, about five to seven minutes, depending on thickness. Drain on paper towels, place on a paper towel-lined platter in a preheated 200°F. oven to keep warm until served.

They taste great plain, but you can also serve them with a cocktail or tartar sauce.

Serves 4.

Flathead catfish.

Fried Kippered Herring

If you like smoked fish and have never tasted kippered herring, you're in for a treat. It's seldom served in the United States, although a good fish market will carry frozen kippers. You find them frequently on menus in Canada and Scotland.

Kippers are fresh herrings which are split, cleaned, then immersed in vats of salt for a few minutes. They are then smoked over oak fires for about eight hours. The result is a distinctively flavored treat. This recipe is simplicity itself. We served it as our fish course in the raffle prize dinner based on a menu from the *Inchcliffe Castle* of Glencannon fame.

Ingredients

2 pkg. frozen Scottish or Canadian kippers (2 fish per package)
2 TBS. butter

Directions

Allow kippers to thaw. Melt butter in a frying pan. Fry kippers for about three minutes on each side. (Fry with the skin side up first so they only have to be turned once.) Remove from pan, cut lengthwise in two so that each serving consists of half a fish. Place on plate, pour remaining butter from pan over fish and serve.

Serves 8.

Herring are cured by soaking in brine and smoking over oak chips for eight hours. The fish are hung in pairs by the tail as pictured at Arbroath, Scotland. Photo: Scottish Tourist Board.

NATIONAL LIBERTY SHIP MEMORIAL

~ *SS JEREMIAH O'BRIEN* ~

MENU
Friday, October 17, 1997

Antipasti
Eggs Diablo

Lettuce Soup O'Brien

Fresh Salad Greens with
Honey-Mustard Dressing

Fileted Truite au bleu

Potatoes Maison
Kernel Corn Escoffier
Carrots Grand Marnier
Buttermilk Crescents

Mocha Roulade Irene
Key Lime Pie

Wines ~ Coffee

Based on the dinner menu for the
SS *Lurline*
Tuesday, December 31, 1957

Matson Lines' Lurline *has also provided many menus that served as a point of departure for our dinners. This was the menu given to our guests for one of that great ship's dinners.*

Truites au Bleu (Blue Trout)

This is a fun recipe because, if done right, the fish turn an interesting blue color. The challenge is in doing it right. Freshly caught, unwashed trout are an absolute must. With store-bought trout you get the flavor but they simply won't turn color. Success depends on not disturbing the natural film that covers the scales. The fish should be touched as little as possible and then only with wet hands on a wet surface. How fresh should they

Ingredients

6 fresh trout
court bouillon
parsley

Court bouillon

4 C. water
¼ C. apple cider vin-
    egar
1 onion
4 whole cloves
2 bay leaves
2 TBS. chopped parsley
8 whole peppercorns

be? Still wriggling when you get them in the kitchen.

Directions

Make the court bouillon by pushing the cloves into the onion and tying it and the remaining ingredients in a piece of cheesecloth. Place in a large pot. Add 4 C. water and the vinegar and bring to a boil over medium high heat. Split each trout lengthwise and clean them. Sprinkle inside and out with vinegar. Plunge them into the vinegar court bouillon, lower heat and simmer for ten minutes. The fish should curl and take on a bluish color. Remove from the liquid and drain well. Serve each fish on a napkin and garnish with a parsley sprig. Serve with a lemon wedge.

Serves 6.

We served this as the fish course based on a *Lurline* menu. I don't know if our guests knew the fish were supposed to be blue, but they weren't. There was too much handling between purchase and the pot. But don't worry, it's a delicious dish, even when it doesn't turn blue.

Peruvian Fish Stew

This dish came about quite by accident. One night I was trying to figure out a way to cook lima beans to have some flavor other than that ordinary tasteless starchiness that limas always have. The beans were planned as a side dish to an entree of fillet of sole. But by combining the two, a meal was created whose flavor, taste and texture was greater than the combination of each of its components — a type of culinary symbiosis. Oh, it was called Peruvian Fish Stew because of the lima beans. Lima is the capital of Peru.

Directions

Wash sole fillets under cold water. Pat dry with paper towels. Sprinkle with salt and pepper and lay on a work surface. In a large skillet or pan, heat white wine, orange peel and orange juice over medium heat. When it just begins to boil, add the Dover sole. Cover, reduce heat to low and cook for about fifteen minutes or until done.

Meanwhile, cook the beans in a small pan according to the directions on the package.

In a medium pan, melt butter over medium heat. Add onion and sauté until the onion just begins to soften and turn

Ingredients

Poached sole

2 lb. Dover sole, filleted
salt
pepper
grated peel of one
   medium size navel
   orange
juice of two medium
   size navel oranges
½ C. white wine

Lima Beans

1 package frozen baby
   lima beans
1 TBS. butter
1 medium sized-onion,
   chopped
½ c. white wine
½ c. water
1 C. tomato sauce
1 clove garlic, chopped
   fine
1 TBS. chopped parsley

NOTE:
It's important not to overcook the onion. The texture of the onion pieces is an important part of this dish. They should be slightly crunchy when served.

golden in color. Add white wine and water. Turn heat to high and reduce the liquid to about ½ cup. Add tomato sauce and reduce heat to low. Simmer for five minutes, add parsley.

Drain the lima beans and mix them with the fish and sauce. Sprinkle with garlic. Serve on plates. If you want a soupier mix, use some of the liquid the fish was poached in and serve in a shallow bowl.

Serves 2

Bev Masterson begins the process of preparing the officers' saloon for one of our raffle prize dinners. Photo: S. Rose.

Poached Salmon with Mousseline Sauce

R.M.S. TITANIC RESTAURANT RECEPTION ROOM

Menu cover from the first class dining room of the RMS Titanic.

No one ever met a salmon they didn't like. Whether it be smoked, pickled, poached, baked, broiled or fried, it's a fish that always pleases. This is another of those recipes from that *Titanic* dinner we did as a raffle prize. By now you probably realize recipes from passenger liners involve a lot of steps and a bit of time in preparation. It's easy to understand why the recipes were so elaborate; "first class" meals on great liners were first class in every sense of the word. In this case the time spent is well worth the effort.

Ingredients

Court bouillon
7 C. water
1 sliced carrot
1 chopped onion
6 peppercorns
1 bay leaf
¼ C. parsley stems
1 tsp. salt
1 ¼ C. dry white wine

Poached Salmon
6 C. court bouillon
6 salmon fillets (8 oz. each)
30 thin slices cucumber
6 sprigs fresh dill

Mousseline Sauce
2/3 C. melted unsalted
   butter
3 TBS. water
3 egg yolks
¼ tsp. each salt and white
   pepper
1 TBS. lemon juice
2 TBS. chopped fresh dill
¼ C. lightly whipped
   cream

Directions

Bring the water, carrot, onion, peppercorns, bay leaf, parsley stems, salt and wine to boil over high heat. Reduce heat and simmer for thirty minutes. Strain.

In a large, shallow pot, heat court bouillon to just below boiling point. Using spatula, place salmon into liquid. If necessary, add enough boiling water to cover. Poach fish until opaque on the outside but still coral-colored in the center (three to five minutes).

Meanwhile, begin the sauce. Skim the froth from the surface of the melted butter and discard. Allow to cool

This dish was appealing to the eye and the taste buds. Our prize winners quickly gobbled it up.

Aldred Chipman chopping onions for this dish and others. Photo: Author.

NOTES:
**1. Since all the vegetables are strained out at the end, you needn't worry about cutting anything too finely.
2. White pepper is one of the few spices worth measuring precisely. It's strong and even a little bit too much will throw off the balance of the sauce.**

slightly. In the top of a double boiler whisk water and egg yolks together with salt and pepper for thirty seconds until pale yellow and frothy. Over barely simmering water, whisk the mixture for three minutes or until it draws a ribbon for five seconds. Remove pan from heat, whisk in warm butter, 1 TBS. at a time until sauce begins to thicken. Still whisking, pour remaining butter into sauce in a slow, steady stream. Stir in lemon and dill. Remove from heat, cool slightly. Gently fold in whipped cream. Adjust seasoning to taste. Keep warm by setting over a pot of warm water.

Arrange salmon on warmed plates. Spoon sauce down center of each piece of fish. Garnish each plate with sliced cucumber and dill sprigs.

Serves 6.

Chinook salmon.

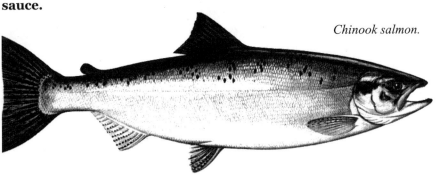

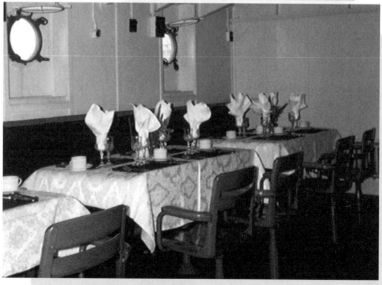

It's an "apples to oranges" comparison, but interesting nontheless. Top, the grand dining room of the great liner Normandie; *center, the Cabin Restaurant of the* Queen Mary; *bottom, the officers' saloon of the* Jeremiah O'Brien. *Our settings are just as elegant and, for a few hours, we try to recreate the experience of the grand liners. Photos: top, Paulus Leeser, center, M.S.E., bottom, Bev Masterson.*

Main Courses

B e it a joint of beef, a pork roast, a brace of ducks or leg of lamb, the main course defines the dinner. Correctly prepared and properly presented, it is what the diner usually remembers best. So, imagine the officers' saloon of the *Jeremiah O'Brien* — tables set with white linen, tall wine glasses filled to the brim, flickering candles casting dancing shadows on the bulkheads and portholes. Wonderful aromas waft gently in from the galley. The appetizer was tantalizing, the soup delightful and the fish course, which was mouth-watering, has been cleared away. You hear your servers approaching and suddenly they appear bearing . . .

After that it's up to you. Read through the following pages and fill in the rest of this fantasy with your own choice. You'll find more of the crew's favorites, the best of our raffle prize dinners and, no doubt, a surprise or two.

Above, thirty-five chefs of the SS France *pose at the bottom of the grand staircase; below, the galley crew of the* Jeremiah O'Brien *pauses while preparing the same type of dinner. It's easy to see by the smiles which group is having the better time. Bottom, left to right, Bev Masterson, Diana Jaffee, Jason Jaffee, author, Aldred Chipman. Photos: top, Compagnie générale maritime; bottom, Wes Masterson.*

Boiled Beef with Hodgils

This was the entrée on our raffle prize dinner based on the Glencannon stories, with a fictional menu created for the SS *Inchcliffe Castle*. Somewhere in the stories is mentioned that fine old British dish, boiled beef. Most Americans envision this as being a chuck roast boiled in a pot of water and think, what a horrid thing to do to a good cut of beef. After digging into it, I discovered the boiled beef in English fare is not fresh, but salted. In fact, the salted joint of beef should be soaked in water overnight, like a Virginia ham, before cooking. Salt beef in any form is almost impossible to find in American markets, so we substituted corned beef (I don't know anyone that doesn't like corned beef) thereby assuring success.

The original recipe for this dish came from Scotland where they do many creative things with oatmeal. The hodgils in this recipe are basically an oatmeal dumpling, an unusual but tasty addition. This is a good dish for the kind of day when the wind is howling, rain beats on the windows and, in your mind's eye, the waves are beating on a rocky coastline.

Ingredients

4 lb. corned beef
1 bay leaf
1½ lb. carrots, peeled and quartered
1 lb. onions, peeled and quartered
3/4 lb. parsnips or turnips (or both), peeled and cubed

For the hodgils

1-1/3 C. oatmeal
1 TBS. chopped chives
salt
pepper

Directions

Figure twenty-five minutes cooking

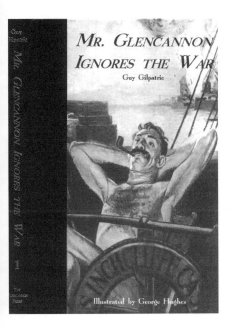

time per pound of meat plus twenty-five
minutes. Put the beef into a pan with the
bay leaf, cover the meat with water and
bring to a boil, covered, over medium
heat. Reduce heat to low. Add vegetables
1½ hours before meat will be done. Mix
the oatmeal with the chives and plenty of
salt and pepper. Use the fat from the top
of the liquid in which the meat is cooking
to bind the oatmeal mixture together.
Roll into balls, making about ten. Let the
hodgils stand for about twenty minutes,
then cook them with the meat for fifteen
minutes. When done, slice the meat, place
the slices on plates surrounded by
vegetables and hodgils. Check the cooking liquid for seasoning and serve as a
gravy.

Serves 8.

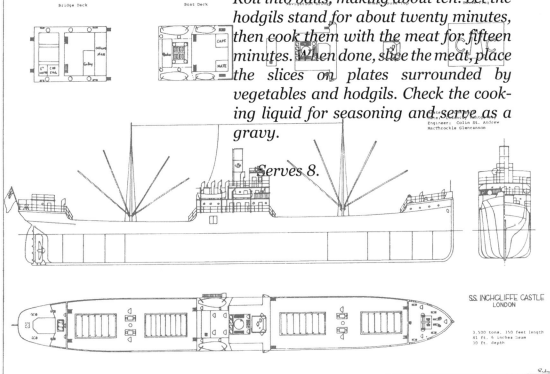

S.S. INCHCLIFFE CASTLE
LONDON

3,500 tons, 150 feet length
41 ft. 6 inches beam
30 ft. depth

Baked Ziti with Spinach and Tomatoes

Here's a good, hardy dish that's easy to prepare and tastes great. It was popular with our ship's crew, so Rich Vannucci talked the Navy volunteer cooks into parting with the recipe.

Directions

Heat a large, heavy saucepan over medium-high heat. Add sausage, onion and garlic and sauté until the sausage is cooked through, breaking up the meat with a spatula, about ten minutes. Add tomatoes, undrained, and simmer until the sauce thickens slightly, stirring occasionally for about ten minutes. Stir in the pesto. Season with salt and pepper. Combine the pasta, spinach, mozzarella and 1/3 C. of the Parmesan cheese in a large bowl. Stir in the hot tomato sauce. Transfer the mixture to a baking dish. Sprinkle the remaining 2/3 C. Parmesan cheese over it. Bake in a 325°F. oven until the sauce bubbles and the cheese melts, about thirty minutes.

Serves 8

Ingredients

1 lb. Italian sausages, casings removed
1 medium onion, chopped
3 garlic cloves, chopped
1-28 oz. can diced, peeled tomatoes
¼ C. pesto sauce (recipe on p. 115)
salt, pepper
10 oz. ziti or penne pasta, cooked
8 C. spinach leaves
6 oz. mozzarella cheese, cubed
1 C. grated Parmesan cheese

Rich Vannucci helping serve the crew breakfast on a Saturday morning. Photo: Author.

Chicken Cacciatore

Chicken is probably one of the most versatile dishes there is — hundreds of recipes exist for its preparation. This is a favorite chicken dish and a crowd-pleaser everywhere, especially on the *Jeremiah O'Brien*. Rich Vannucci again brings his Italian heritage to the fore, giving us a dish that can't be improved upon. I guarantee there will be no leftovers on this one.

Ingredients

3 lb. chicken, cut into 8 serving pieces
salt and pepper
¼ C. olive oil
2 medium onions, sliced
4 cloves garlic, minced
1 green pepper, seeds removed and chopped medium
½ C. sauterne wine
1 TBS. red wine vinegar
½ C. chicken stock
3 fresh tomatoes, peeled, seeded and chopped
1 tsp. oregano
½ C. finely chopped, fresh rosemary
1 bay leaf
½ lb. mushrooms, thickly sliced
1 C. Greek cured olives, with pits
½ C. chopped parsley

Directions

Heat oil in pan over medium heat. Meanwhile season chicken with salt and pepper. Brown chicken on all sides and remove to a dish. Add onions, garlic and green pepper. Sauté for eight minutes. Transfer to the dish with the chicken. Add wine and vinegar and boil until reduced by half. Add chicken stock and boil a moment longer. Return chicken and onion mixture to the pan. Add tomatoes, oregano, rosemary and bay leaf. Cover and simmer for thirty minutes. Add mushrooms and olives and cook fifteen minutes longer. Season, remove bay leaf and garnish with parsley.

Serves 4-6.

Chicken Jambalaya

Jambalaya is basically a Cajun rice dish that traces its ancestry to Spanish *paella*. Because one of the key ingredients is ham and the French word for ham is *jambón,* it is believed the name of the dish is a Cajunized version of the French word. Although we served this as an entrée in our *Creole Queen* raffle prize dinner, you can prepare it as a one dish meal. There are plenty of vegetables and seasonings for everyone. Consider doubling the recipe. There will be calls for seconds.

Directions

Heat the oil over high heat in a heavy, 7 or 8 qt. quart kettle. Brown the chicken parts in the hot oil, turning them occasionally to ensure even browning. As the pieces brown, remove them to a platter. When all the chicken is browned and removed, add the vegetables, garlic, parsley, ham and pork to the pot. Reduce the heat to medium and cook, stirring frequently for about fifteen minutes or until the meat and vegetables are browned. Add the sausage and the seasonings, cooking and stirring for another five minutes, then add the reserved chicken parts, the rice and the water. Mix gently. Raise the heat to high

Ingredients

2 TBS. vegetable oil
1 frying chicken, 3 to 4 lb., cut up, rinsed and dried
4 C. chopped onion
3/4 C. chopped green pepper
3/4 C. thinly sliced scallion tops
1 TBS. minced garlic
3 TBS. finely minced fresh parsley
½ C. finely chopped lean baked ham
1 lb. lean pork, cut into ½-inch cubes
6 smoked sausages (Creole, Polish, Garlic) sliced ½-inch thick and refrigerated
3½ tsp. salt
½ tsp. freshly ground black pepper
¼ tsp. cayenne
½ tsp. chili powder
2 whole bay leaves, crushed
¼ tsp. dried thyme
1/8 tsp. cloves
¼ tsp. dried basil
1/8 tsp. mace
1½ C. long grain white rice
3 C. water

NOTE:
Contrary to normal practice, in this case you want a fat frying chicken. The fat is a key ingredient in flavoring the entire dish. Remember, fat is flavor.

and bring the mixture to a boil, then cover the pot and lower the heat to as low as possible. Cook for forty-five minutes, stirring occasionally. Uncover during the last ten minutes of cooking and raise the heat to medium. Stir gently and frequently as the rice dries out. Serve immediately.

Serves 6-8.

Samuel Clemens' (Mark Twain) original Mississippi River pilot's license The Mariner's Museum.

Georgian Lamb Stew

BLACK SEA

Georgia

We haven't yet served this dish on the *Jeremiah O'Brien*, but we will some day, when we do a Russian dinner. Good for cold, rainy days when you want something simple to warm your insides. The excellent taste comes as quite a surprise because the preparation is so simple. The "Georgia" in this dish, by the way, is not in the United States, but in the former Soviet Union.

Directions

Remove the lamb from the bone and cut into 3/4 inch cubes, leaving any visible fat on the meat. In a large kettle, cook the lamb over low heat, stirring occasionally, for ten minutes or until no longer pink. Add onion and cook over moderately low heat, stirring occasionally until the onion is soft. Add the tomatoes, the potatoes and a pinch of salt. Simmer the mixture, covered, occasionally stirring, for forty minutes or until the potatoes are tender. Mix in the herbs and cayenne and simmer for four minutes. Stir in the garlic and remove the stew from the heat. Let stand covered for five minutes. Season with salt and pepper.

Serves 4.

Ingredients

1½ lb. lamb from the wide end of a leg of lamb with bone in, or 1½ lbs. lamb steak with the bone in
1 large onion
1 lb. canned plum tomatoes, or 1 lb. fresh
2 boiling potatoes (about 1 3/4 lb.), cut into ½-inch dice, simmered in salt water for 1 minute and drained
½ C. loosely packed mixture of coriander leaves, fresh mint, leaves, fresh basil leaves, fresh dill sprigs and fresh parsley coarsely chopped together
½ tsp. cayenne
4 large minced garlic cloves
salt and pepper

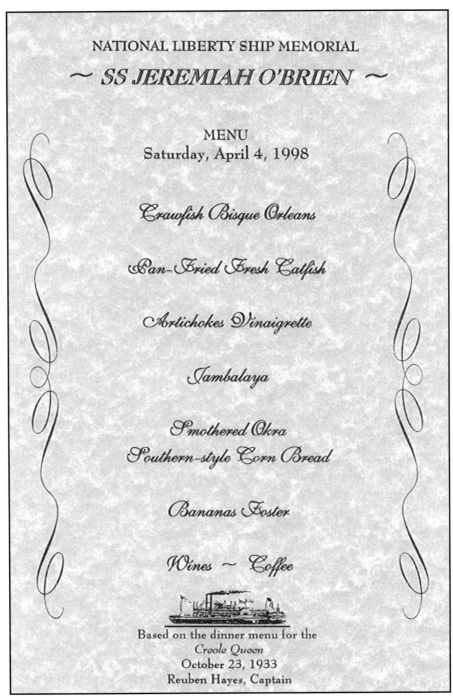

NATIONAL LIBERTY SHIP MEMORIAL

~ *SS JEREMIAH O'BRIEN* ~

MENU
Saturday, April 4, 1998

Crawfish Bisque Orleans

Pan-Fried Fresh Catfish

Artichokes Vinaigrette

Jambalaya

Smothered Okra
Southern-style Corn Bread

Bananas Foster

Wines ~ Coffee

Based on the dinner menu for the
Creole Queen
October 23, 1933
Reuben Hayes, Captain

Louisiana cooking was featured on this menu based on the paddlewheel steamer Creole Queen.

Layered Enchiladas

Bev Masterson, who is such an important part of these dinners, provided a favorite recipe for this book. It's unusual because the tortillas are cut in half and layered with the other ingredients, rather than being rolled.

Directions

In a large frying pan over medium heat, brown the beef and chorizo. Drain the fat. Add oregano, cumin, cayenne, garlic, salt and pepper.

Meanwhile, put the chili sauce in a large sauce pan over medium heat. Mix flour and water to form a paste and slowly add to the chili sauce to thicken. Simmer until the sauce has a consistency of thin batter.

Cut the tortillas in half. Pour enough chili sauce in a casserole dish to cover the bottom. Place a layer of tortillas on the sauce (after dipping in remaining sauce). Cover tortillas with a layer of meat, onion, cheese and olives, then sprinkle with Parmesan cheese. Put enough sauce on this layer to moisten. Repeat until ingredients are used up, finishing with a layer of sauce topped with Parmesan cheese. Bake at 350°F. until bubbles appear, about thirty minutes.

Serves 6-8.

Ingredients

1 can Las Palmas Chili sauce
12 flour tortillas
1 lb. ground beef
½ lb. Mexican chorizo sausage, casings removed
1 TBS. oregano
1 TBS ground cumin
¼ tsp. cayenne
4 cloves garlic, chopped fine
salt
black pepper
2 TBS. white flour
¼ C. water
1 onion, grated
6 oz. cheddar cheese, grated
1 C. black olives, chopped
6 oz. Parmesan cheese, grated

Lemon Chicken

Ingredients

2 large chickens, quartered, fat and skin removed

Marinade

1 C. fresh squeezed lemon juice
1 C. sauterne wine
1/3 C. fresh rosemary, finely chopped
3 cloves garlic, finely chopped
dash of cumin
salt & pepper
1/3 C. olive oil.

NOTE:
Fresh rosemary is the key ingredient. The dried type tends to impart a slightly bitter flavor when used in large quantities.

Mariners are, in general, an adventurous lot and they become acquainted with cuisine from all over. Rich Vannucci, of the *O'Brien*'s galley crew, has collected recipes from many of the countries he visited while in the Navy. This recipe is from Thrace, in Greece, and the ship's crew says it's quite good.

Directions

In a large bowl, mix marinade. Add chicken, coating each piece. Marinate for two hours. Place chicken, meaty side up, in a shallow baking pan. Bake for thirty minutes in a preheated 375°F. oven.

Serves 8.

Lobscouse

This traditional seafaring stew traces its roots to the Norwegian *brun lapskaus* or Swedish *lapskaus* and was originally a stew of salt meat and hard tack boiled together with pepper. If the cook was in a generous mood he might throw in a few potatoes. And, in the first couple of weeks after sailing, an onion or two might find its way into the meal. You often see the name of this dish shortened to "scouse" as did Richard Henry Dana in *Two Years Before the Mast*. In time, lobscouse evolved with additional ingredients to the dish found today in New England, Nova Scotia and as served on merchant ships up until containerization changed the industry.

Directions

Soak the meat for twelve hours to remove the salt. Cook the meat in seven cups of water for one hour. Add the vegetables, rice and peppercorns. Cook until the vegetables are tender, stirring occasionally, about forty-five minutes.

Serves 8.

NOTE: Salt meat is not commonly found in markets or even delicatessens. If

Ingredients

1 lb. salt meat cubed
1 med. onion
2 TBS. rice
1 C. each chopped
   carrots, turnips,
   potatoes
1 diced parsnip
1 C. chopped cabbage
6 peppercorns

THE HARVARD CLASSICS
EDITED BY CHARLES W. ELIOT, LL.D.

Two Years Before the Mast

AND TWENTY-FOUR YEARS AFTER

By R. H. Dana, Jr.

With Introduction and Notes

P. F. Collier & Son Corporation
NEW YORK

you're determined to use salt meat, buy a cheap cut of beef, rub it with pickling salt and let it cure in a cool, dry place for a month or so. Check it occasionally and add salt as needed.

Or, substitute corned beef for the salt meat in the recipe, in which case omit soaking it ahead of time.

One additional suggestion: sailing ship cooks used broken up hard tack to absorb some of the liquid and thicken the dish. You can accomplish the same thing by breaking up a few saltine crackers and throwing them in.

The leftovers make an excellent breakfast hash. Drain most of the liquid and fry the leftovers in a tablespoon of olive oil.

Lobscouse originated on Scandinavian ships. The Herzogin Cecile, *under the flag of Finland, was the flagship of Gustaf Erikson's fleet. Photo: Mansell collection.*

Marinated Flank Steak

Wes and Bev Masterson are two of the most dedicated *O'Brien* volunteers. In the ship's normal routine Wes works in the deck department and Bev manages the *O'Brien*'s gift shop. They also help with the raffle prize dinners. Wes is one of those people who is always there when you need him — whether it be to chop onions, stir something on the stove, help set the tables, or clean up afterward. He is also a cook in his own right. This is his recipe for a great barbecue dish.

Ingredients

2 lb. flank steak
½ C. melted butter
½ C. honey
1/3 C. vinegar
1/3 C. vegetable oil
3 TBS. soy sauce
3 TBS. Worcestershire Sauce
4 cloves garlic, chopped medium
8 scallions, chopped medium
salt
pepper

Directions

Mix all the ingredients together. Place in a glass bowl with the steak, cover and marinate, refrigerated for twelve hours or overnight. Turn occasionally. Barbecue about four inches from coals to desired doneness. Cut in strips to serve.

Serves 4 to 6.

Bev and Wes Masterson wearing Jeremiah O'Brien *souvenir sweater and polo shirt. Photo: Courtesy Bev Masterson.*

Time Capsule

D-Day, 1944

On June 2, 1944 the SS Jeremiah O'Brien *departed Scotland and sailed down the Irish Sea toward Land's End and the English Channel. At every port naval vessels joined the fleet. The convoy was covered by a heavy escort of ships and by an umbrella of Spitfires, Hurricanes, B-24s and Mosquitos. Merchant Mariners aboard the* O'Brien *remembered: "You never saw so many ships. Thousands, just thousands and thousands, it was incredible ... The* Jeremiah O'Brien *was at the head of the convoy, in the first wave of ships ... as far as you could see, for mile after mile in the distance, ships, ships, ships! ... There were so many ships that the curvature of the earth prevented you from seeing it all. It was just stupendous!"*

June 5. The O'Brien *was anchored outside the Solent of Southampton loaded with army troops for the invasion of Normandy. Throughout the night hundreds and thousands of planes passed overhead. Allied bombardment of the French coast had started. The glare was visible from across the Channel. No one slept. It was D-Day, Tuesday, June 6, 1944.*

The Last Liberty (1993)
Walter W. Jaffee

The O'Brien *made eleven Normandy landings. In June 1994 she returned for the 50th Anniversary of D-Day. She was the only ship from the great armada to return and was a "guest of honor" at the ceremonies.*

Roast Duckling With Orange Sauce (Caneton à l'Orange ou à la Bigarade)

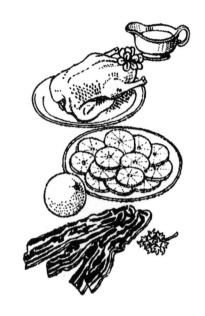

One popular menu we did was from a 1969 cruise of the *President Roosevelt*, the American President Lines around-the-world passenger ship. An entrée from the May 20th menu was Breast of Duck With Orange Sauce. We featured that menu and served this dish, using the whole duck, not just the breast, for one of our raffle prize dinners on the *Jeremiah O'Brien*. Aldred Chipman, who also cooks on most of these dinners, was able to get some fresh ducks from San Francisco's Chinatown. The rest, as they say, is history.

Directions

With a damp cloth, wipe the duckling and prick all over with a fork. Rub with salt and pepper. Roast in a 400°F. oven for fifteen minutes. Lower the temperature to 350°F. and continue to roast, allowing 20 minutes per pound. Baste frequently with the white wine.

In a small pan, melt the sugar and blend in the vinegar until it caramelizes. Remove the duck from the oven and the roasting pan. Cover with foil to keep warm. Skim the fat from the roasting pan and slowly add the chicken broth to the remaining liquid, scraping the loose

Ingredients

5-6 lb. duckling
salt
pepper
1 C. dry white wine

For the sauce:

1 TBS. sugar
1 TBS. red wine vinegar
1 C. chicken broth
Juice of four oranges
Juice of one lemon.
2 TBS. brandy

Peel of one orange for garnish.
Two sliced, blanched oranges for garnish

Sharp knives are essential to any successful cooking effort. Photo: S. Rose.

bits from the bottom of the pan as you do so. Blend in the orange juice, lemon juice, brandy and vinegar caramel. Cook slowly for ten minutes.

Arrange the duck on a large heated platter, pour the sauce over it and sprinkle the orange rinds on top. Surround the duck with the blanched orange slices.

Serves 4.

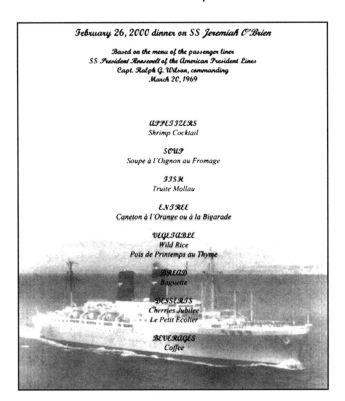

February 26, 2000 dinner on SS *Jeremiah O'Brien*

Based on the menu of the passenger liner
SS *President Roosevelt* of the American President Lines
Capt. Ralph G. Wilson, commanding
March 20, 1969

APPETIZERS
Shrimp Cocktail

SOUP
Soupe à l'Oignon au Fromage

FISH
Truite Mollau

ENTREE
Caneton à l'Orange ou à la Bigarade

VEGETABLE
Wild Rice
Pois de Printemps au Thyme

BREAD
Baguette

DESSERTS
Cherries Jubilee
Le Petit Ecolier

BEVERAGES
Coffee

Roast Leg of Lamb with Mint Sauce

This was the main course for our *Titanic* dinner and, again, *Last Dinner on the* Titanic was, with a few changes, our guide. Lamb is probably the least used meat commonly available. The taste is distinctive, the aroma while it is cooking, divine. The trick with this dish is to make your own mint sauce. If you buy the bottled stuff you might as well throw this book away. Another hint: if possible, use fresh lamb rather than frozen and make some effort to get fresh herbs. It makes a big difference.

Directions

Trim gristle and excess fat. Stir together garlic, 2 TBS. of the oil, rosemary, mustard and pepper; rub over surface of the meat, marinate at room temperature for at least an hour or in a refrigerator for up to forty-eight hours. In a large, heavy skillet, heat the remaining oil over high heat; add lamb and sear, turning often, until browned all over (about five minutes).

Place leg in roasting pan. Deglaze the skillet by pouring wine and salt into it; bring to boil, stirring to scrape up any brown bits; pour over meat. Cook lamb in 450°F. oven for fifteen minutes, reduce

Ingredients

1 leg of lamb (approx. 4 lb.)
2 cloves garlic, minced
3 TBS. olive oil
2 TBS. chopped fresh rosemary
1 tsp. Dijon mustard
2 tsp. freshly ground pepper
1/4 C. white wine
½ tsp. salt

Mint Sauce

2 minced shallots
¼ C. white wine
1 C. chicken stock
2 tsp. cider vinegar
1 tsp. granulated sugar
1/4 C. fresh mint
Fresh mint sprigs

NOTES:

1. **If you like garlic, take a couple of extra cloves, cut them into slivers, poke holes in the lamb with a knife tip and insert the garlic before roasting.**
2. **The lamb actually continues cooking after you take it out and tent it with foil.**
3. **Allowing the meat to rest before slicing causes it to hold together better when you slice it. Otherwise it has a tendency to fall apart. Also, it gives the juices a chance to reabsorb, rather than drain.**
4. **If you like sauce on your meat, double the sauce ingredients. That way you're sure of having enough.**
5. **Personally, I like all the little bits and pieces in the sauce. You don't really *have* to sieve it.**

heat to 350°F. for another twenty-five minutes for rare, thirty-five minutes for medium-rare. Remove lamb from pan, tent with foil, and let rest for fifteen minutes.

Mint Sauce: Meanwhile, place roasting pan over medium heat. Stir in shallots and cook, stirring often, for five minutes or until softened. Stir in wine, bring to boil and cook, stirring for one minute or until reduced to a glaze. Stir in the stock, vinegar and sugar. Continue to boil rapidly for two minutes or until sauce is slightly thickened; pour through fine-meshed sieve. Stir in mint. Serve sauce alongside roast. Garnish with fresh mint sprigs.

Serves 6.

The RMS Titanic *as she appeared before launching. Photo:* Liners, the Golden Age.

Roast Pork with Sage and Onion Stuffing

Pork, like lamb, is often underrated. Especially as a roast. There is nothing quite like a juicy pork roast with a crispy skin on it. I know, the cholesterol in the skin is bad for you, but surely once in a while won't hurt.

We did this as the entrée for our Patrick O'Brian Night raffle prize dinner. Recreating a shipboard menu from a British man-o'-war in the early 1800s was a lot of fun. You could almost see the oil lanterns swaying in the saloon as the ship slowly made its way across a gently rolling sea and the officers drank a toast to the king before sitting down to dinner.

Our main mistake was not to baste the roast as it was cooking, so the skin came out a bit on the dry side. "Liver and loin" (live and learn) as they say.

Ingredients

8 lb. leg of pork with skin
flour
1 TBS. fresh sage

Sage and Onion Stuffing

1 large onion, peeled
2 TBS. fresh sage
1 C. stale French bread, crumbled
1 tsp. dry mustard
1 egg
salt
pepper

Directions

First, make the stuffing. Blanch the onion in boiling water for 5 minutes. Add the sage and cook thirty seconds longer. Strain and chop coarsely. Add the bread, mustard, egg and salt and pepper to taste. Mix well.

Bone the roast. Sew it together leaving a pocket for the stuffing. Spoon the stuffing into the pocket and sew it

closed. (At this point, if you are going to spit roast it, tie the whole thing up with butcher's twine so it doesn't fall apart as it cooks. Otherwise, place it in a roasting pan.) *Dredge with flour and place in a 325°F. oven (or on a spit over a fire). After one hour, remove roast and score the skin in 1-inch squares. Tear the sage in small pieces and insert into the cut skin. Return the meat to the fire or oven and roast, basting occasionally, for another 2 hours or until a meat thermometer reads 160°F. Place on a platter, covered with foil, and let rest for fifteen minutes. Carve and serve.*

Serves 10

Officers of the British Navy toast the coming battle of Trafalgar with Admiral Nelson. National Maritime Museum, Greenwich, England.

Veal Picatta

We did an Italian night for one of our *Jeremiah O'Brien* raffle prize dinners based on a 1933 menu from the cargo-passenger liner *President Harrison*. I wanted to serve veal picatta as the entree, but had the darndest time locating a recipe. In the end we adapted another Italian veal dish, adding some lemon and capers for that "picatta" flavor. It worked. There weren't any leftovers.

Directions

Season the scallops with salt and pepper, dip in flour and shake off the excess. In a heavy skillet melt 2 TBS. of butter with the olive oil over moderate heat. When the foam subsides, add the veal, four or five scallops at a time, and sauté them for two minutes on each side or until golden brown. Transfer to a plate. Pour off all but a thin film of fat from the skillet. Add ½ C. beef stock and boil briskly for about two minutes, stirring constantly and scraping in any browned bits clinging to the pan. Return the veal to the skillet and arrange the lemon slices on top. Cover and simmer over low heat for ten to fifteen minutes or until tender. Transfer to a heated platter and surround with the lemon slices. Add

Ingredients

1½ lbs. veal scallops, cut 3/8 inch thick and pounded until ¼ inch thick (or buy them already cut to the size you want)
salt
pepper
flour
4 TBS. butter
3 TBS. olive oil
3/4 C. beef stock
6 thin lemon slices
1 TBS. lemon juice
1 TBS. capers

Aldred Chipman brings many fine qualities to our raffle prize dinners: great cooking skills, a wry sense of humor, the occasional Liberty Ale — and he can find the most esoteric ingredients. Photo: S. Rose.

the remaining beef stock to the juices in the skillet and boil until the stock is reduced to a syrupy glaze. Add the lemon juice and cook, stirring, for one minute. Remove pan from heat, swirl in the remaining butter and pour over the scallops. Garnish with capers.

Serves 4.

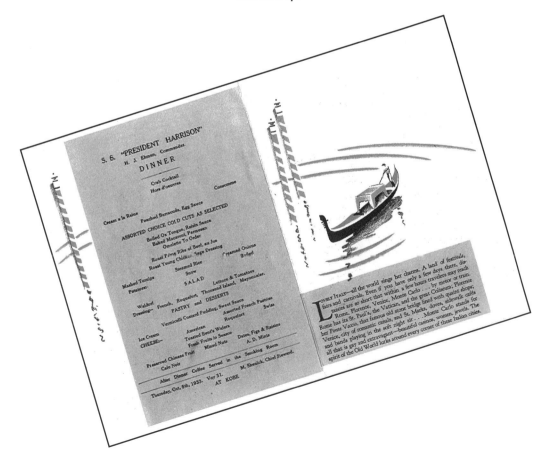

Veal Schnitzel Holstein

One of type of cooking we don't have trouble with on the *O'Brien*'s coal-fired stove is sautéing or frying. Temperature control is simply a matter of lifting the frying pan off the stove when it gets too hot.

This recipe is a lot of fun because it involves the use of the ship's humongous industrial-sized frying pan. It's about two feet across and has a handle that you almost need two hands to lift. What's fun about it is that the cook can be a little flamboyant, sliding the pan from one place to another on the stove, flipping and tossing stuff here and there as if he knew what he was doing.

Schnitzel is usually thought of as being Austrian or German, and this recipe probably originated in the Schleswig-Holstein area of Germany, just below the Danish border. It makes a dramatic presentation when done right.

Directions

Sprinkle the veal with salt and pepper, dredge in flour. Dip each scallop into lightly beaten egg and coat it with fine dry bread crumbs. Melt butter in frying pan over high heat and sauté the meat for about three minutes on each

Ingredients

6 veal scallops
salt
pepper
2 eggs
1 C. bread crumbs
6 TBS. butter
6 eggs
anchovy fillets for
  garnish
capers for garnish

NOTE:
It's best to get the veal already cut into scallops so you don't have to pound it.

The Holstein cow originated in Holland. Photo: Encyclopedia Britannica.

side, until the crumbs are golden colored. Place each schnitzel on a plate, top with a fried egg. Place anchovy fillets in an X shape over the yolk of each egg. Sprinkle with capers and serve.

Serves 6.

This dish is so good it's one of the few that's been repeated in our shipboard dinners.

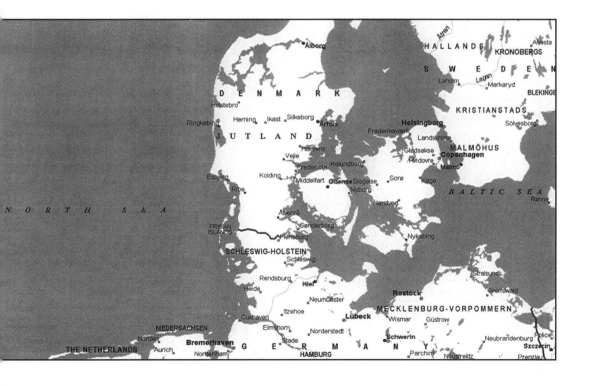

Tortilla Casserole

Our 1994 voyage to Normandy was crewed by volunteers. Because it lasted almost six months many of them couldn't make the entire voyage. Those that did had seniority over those that didn't. All three cooks on the voyage made the entire trip. Joe Guzzetta joined the galley crew during the later part of the voyage and, because the cooks berths were already taken, his talents were used in other ways. It is only recently that his skill as a cook has come forth. But now he has plenty of opportunity. His Tortilla Casserole is a crew favorite, especially on those cold, foggy San Francisco days of late summer.

Directions

Coat an 11x14 roasting pan with the olive oil. Set aside. Brown the meat, onion and chili powder together in a large skillet over medium heat. Add corn, olives and one can of soup. Cover the bottom of the roasting pan with eight tortillas, overlapping as necessary. Cover with one-third of the meat mixture then one-third of the cheese. Repeat twice more. On the last layer, pour the remaining can of soup over the top, then add the cheese. Cover with foil and bake in a pre-heated 375°F. oven for forty-five to fifty minutes.

Serves 6-10

Ingredients

2 lb. ground beef
4 large onions, chopped coarse
4 TBS. chili powder
2 small cans chopped black olives, drained
2 medium cans corn, drained
2 cans Campbell's tomato soup
4 C. cheddar cheese, grated
¼ C. olive oil
24 tortillas

Joe Guzzetta is a veteran of our voyage to Normandy and an accomplished cook. Photo: Courtesy Rich Vannucci.

Vermicelli with Pesto Sauce

Ingredients

Vermicelli for four (you can use any spaghetti-type pasta)

Pesto Sauce

3 garlic cloves
2 TBS. chopped basil leaves
2 TBS. freshly grated Parmesan cheese
1 TBS. pine nuts
¼ tsp. salt
3 TBS. olive oil

NOTES:
1. **You can substitute walnuts for the pine nuts, and commercial (canned) cheese for fresh, but it won't be as good.**
2. **Also, you can double, triple or increase the recipe for the sauce in any amount, just keep the proportions the same.**

This traditional Italian dish came from a December 1958 menu on the passenger liner *Mariposa*. Before the age of jet planes, Matson liners were the most popular way to get to Hawaii from the U. S. West Coast. The luxury of relaxing for five days en route to Honolulu is now lost and I think we're worse off for it. We tried to recapture some of the elegance of that era with our *Mariposa* raffle prize dinner. The dish is simple, the key to its success is fresh ingredients in the correct proportions.

Directions
For the pasta:
Add the pasta to boiling water to which you've added 1 tsp. olive oil and ½ tsp. salt. Cook until just done or "al dente" (about fifteen minutes).

For the sauce:
Purée the garlic, basil, cheese, nuts, salt and olive oil in a blender.

Serves 4.

First, Take Two-and-a-half Tons of Turkey ...

A unique type of maritime cooking was aboard troopships. Replaced in modern times by the jumbo jet, these massive vessels were once the only means of getting large numbers of soldiers from one place to another. Carrying 5,000 or more each leg of each voyage, their galley crews (small armies in themselves) specialized in producing functional food — "three squares a day," as they say. The *Jeremiah O'Brien* carried hundreds of Army troops during the Normandy landings, but because of the unique circumstances, few meals were prepared. The other regular troopships, however, did cook and serve unimaginably vast quantities of food around the clock.

The following is a glimpse at what it takes for "Dinner for 5,000," from an article by the author published some years ago.

"An army travels on its stomach," said Napoleon. The mental image conjured up by this phrase is usually long lines of olive-drab-colored trucks full of unappetizing cardboard boxes. Eventually, at the end of the line is the soldier, eating K-rations out of a mess kit, or bravely trying to heat a can of stew in his helmet over a fire. But, before the soldier ever got to the end of that line he was already "traveling on his stomach."

The difficulties of feeding servicemen while traveling are all but forgotten. Today troops move from one place to another by jet. Feeding them involves simply having on hand and serving one or two pre-packaged meals (MRE or Meal, Ready to Eat). Before airplanes, however, there were ships.

The busiest time of transporting soldiers by ship was during World War II. Five thousand troops would be on board for as long as twenty-five days, each way. Pity the poor chief steward whose job it was to feed these people, plus the ship's crew of over 400, and have it all work out ... somehow.

The ship itself was usually up to the job. Many of them were twin-stack P-2's built for the express purpose of carrying troops.

The troopship General William Mitchell *operated for the Military Sea Transport Service (later Military Sealift Command) until the 1960s. Photo: National Archives.*

In fact, the design was so good it was used in later years for luxury passenger ships such as American President Lines' *President Cleveland* and *President Wilson*.

The P-2's were ideally laid out with proper galleys and storage space although the mess rooms weren't quite up to the standards of passenger liners. Picnic style tables with benches and stainless steel trays and utensils were how the average GI received his "haute cuisine."

To help in his planning, the chief steward had at his disposal "the Menu Guide ... Prepared for Use on Transports." Written by the Army Service Forces, San Francisco Port of Embarkation, in October of 1944, it was Betty Crocker and Julia Child to the transport cook. In addition to explaining how to create a varied menu three times a day for thirty days, and providing recipes for creative cookery, it also explained the philosophy of cooking, all in perfect "militarese."

"A satisfactory menu is well-balanced, provides variety and pleasing food combination, and is within the authorized ration allowance.

"A satisfactory menu will become unsatisfactory when the food is improperly handled and cooked. Careless handling and cooking may cause partial or complete loss of vitamins and minerals naturally present and essential to the maintenance of good health."

The head chef on the *QEII* might claim there's a lot more to satisfactory menu planning than that.

As to the actual preparing and cooking of food, the guide had this to say:

"The ration of the American soldier is the best in the world in quality, quantity, and variety of food delivered."

Thousands of seasoned troops might challenge *that* statement.

"Cooking is the art of preparing food for human consumption. This includes the all-important phase of initial washing, cutting, peeling, etc., of the raw products, and the actual application of heat to the food, when necessary, to improve its palatability and digestibility and to destroy any disease germs that may be present.

"The American soldier, while not requiring heavy energy when traveling by water, has nevertheless, formed the habit of eating three meals a day on shore, his stomach is just as large and the sea air tends to increase his appetite. Three good meals a day will be a great help in maintaining a high standard of morale and the physical fitness of the troops lifted."

Troop ships were concerned with Basic Cooking. They carried one herb — 550 bunches of fresh parsley — and this was probably for garnish.

"The success of a meal, to the coffee drinker, and most soldiers are coffee drinkers, depends upon the quality of the beverage served. The making of good coffee with proper flavor, aroma, and body or 'cup quality' is an art that must be mastered by the cook."

Brewing a good cup of coffee *is* an art. Most of us manage a pot for ten or twelve. Imagine brewing coffee for 5,500 people at a time. Starting with several large cauldrons, you first add 236 gallons of cold water. Into the strainer baskets divide proportionally 118 pounds of

The twin-stack General Alexander E. Anderson. *Original plans for this type called for conversion to United States Lines passenger liners after World War II. The plans never came to fruition. Photo: National Archives.*

The General Nelson M. Walker *was a slightly different model than the two preceeding. The last two ships of this class became the* President Wilson *and* President Cleveland. *Photo: National Archives.*

coffee. To insure "cup quality," throw in an extra third of a pound. "Apply heat" and you have coffee for breakfast. Repeat the process at each meal.

The menus themselves make fascinating reading. Day twenty-one of the thirty day menu reads as follows:

Breakfast
Oranges
Cereal, cornmeal
Sausage, pork
Eggs, scrambled
Cornbread
Butter, apple
Coffee

Lunch
Salad, coleslaw
Cold meats, assorted
Bread, fresh

Butter
Jam
Juice, pineapple

Dinner
Olives, ripe
Turkey, roast
Dressing
Sauce, cranberry
Potatoes, mashed
Asparagus, melted butter
Peas, green
Ice Cream
Cookies
Bread, fresh
Butter
Coffee

It was a reasonably good menu the GI could look forward to. To prepare the above dishes, the following ingredients were needed

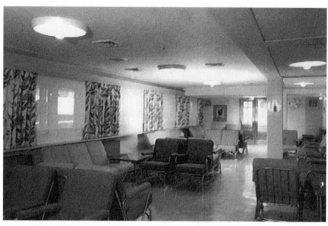

The officers' and dependents lounge on the General William O. Darby *shows there was some degree of luxury and comfort found on troopships. Photo: National Archives.*

just to feed the troops, not to mention the ship's crew of over 400:

5,000 pounds of turkey
400 pounds of luncheon meat
400 pounds of sausage, bologna
400 pounds of sausage, liver
1,250 pounds of sausage, pork link
800 dozen eggs
1,200 cans of milk, evap.
200 gallons of ice cream
400 pounds of butter
50 #10 cans of apple butter
75 #10 cans of jam
350 pounds of coffee
750 pounds of sugar
700 pounds of cookies, assorted
350 pounds of cornmeal, yellow
500 #10 cans of pineapple juice
5,000 oranges. fresh
100 #10 cans of sauce, cranberry
150 #10 cans of asparagus
150 #10 cans of peas, green
1,000 pounds of cabbage, fresh
50 pounds of peppers, green
2,750 pounds of potatoes, Irish
250 pounds of onions
25 #10 cans of olives, ripe

Plus horseradish, mustard. salt, pepper, and other condiments.

Imagine what a workday is like for the cook who must prepare all that. Opening the door to the galley in the early morning, he is greeted by a mountain of frozen turkey, several alpine-sized piles of various sausages, a few hills of cans and bags, and here and there a mound of cabbage, a hillock of oranges, a pile of onions. Behind him, in his mind's ear, he can already hear the 5,000 GI's clamoring for food. His crew is a small army in itself. They begin mixing dough for bread and batter for cakes — hundreds of pounds at a time in mixers the size of backyard cement mixers. Ovens and grills and vent fans are turned on, after calling the engine room to warn them to put an extra generator on the line to handle the power surge. Miles of breakfast sausages are grilled, eggs are scrambled by the gross, the coffee is made. While breakfast is still being served, loaves of bread by the hundreds are baked for later in the day, cold-cuts by the yard are sliced, dressings and sauces by the gallon for dinner are begun. Later the turkeys are roasted, potatoes peeled by the hundredweight, boiled and mashed, and the dinner vegetables heated. Vats of soups or vegetables are stirred with paddles large enough to row a canoe. The proportions are huge, everything in hundreds and thousands.

And that's just for one day.

For further guidance, the chief steward was given recipes to some of the most difficult dishes.

Cake, chocolate

Ingredients:

>   675 lbs. flour
>   300 lbs. sugar
>   200 cans milk, evaporated
>   175 lbs. lard substitute
>   50 lbs. cocoa
>   33 lbs. eggs, dry
>   31 lbs. 4 oz. baking powder
>   6 lbs. 2 oz. salt

Bread, white

Ingredients:

>   1,250 lbs. flour
>   800 lbs. (yes, pounds) water
>   31 lbs. yeast, compressed
>   31 lbs. salt
>   50 lbs. sugar
>   70 lbs. shortening
>   56 lbs. milk, dry

Unfortunately, the guide doesn't tell the cook how to prepare the recipes. One can only hope he was trained before he signed on.

The average round trip voyage took between six weeks and two months so troopships carried supplies for sixty days. To do so required 11,000 cubic feet of chill storage, 7,500 cubic feet of ventilated storage and 25,000 cubic feet of dry storage. This is equivalent to filling four average three-bedroom, two-bath homes from floor to ceiling.

A sample of what went in these spaces is formidable, 12½ tons of frozen bacon, 5 tons of hamburger (this was before the days of the quarter-pounder), 880 gallons of ice cream, 6½ tons of frozen halibut 5½ tons of frozen turkey, 82 tons of potatoes, 120,000 fresh oranges, 11 tons of fresh turnips, 50,000 dozen fresh eggs, 850 pounds of dried eggs, 14 tons of carrots, 9 tons of onions, 5,000 bottles of catsup, 1,500 pounds of cocoa, 10 tons of coffee, 1,300 cans of chili without beans, 110 bottles of vanilla extract, 440 pounds of garlic, and 30 tons of sugar, just to mention a few.

There was an additional problem on troopships. Suppose you prepare dinner for 5,000, the weather gets bad and only half of them decide to eat. What do you do with a ton of left-over turkey; half a ton of left-over potatoes, mashed; and seventy-five already opened #10 cans of already cooked peas, green?

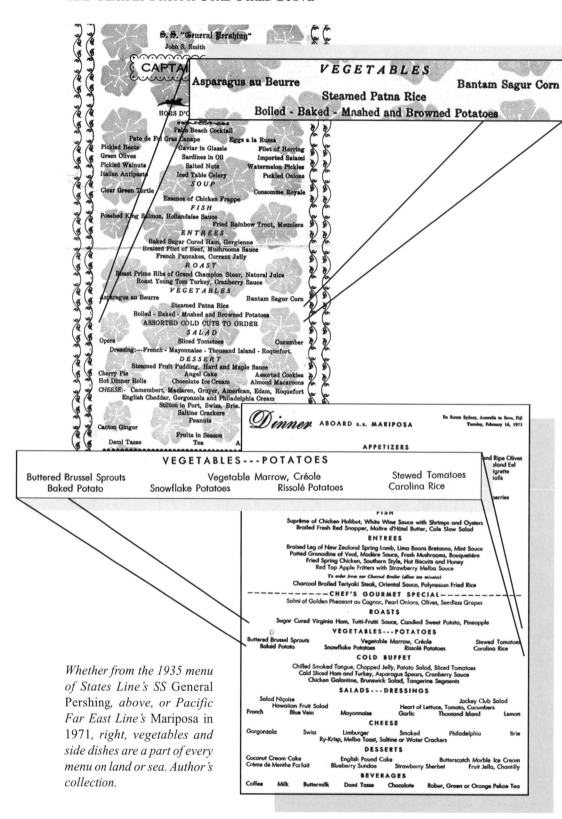

Whether from the 1935 menu of States Line's SS General Pershing, *above, or Pacific Far East Line's* Mariposa *in 1971,* right, *vegetables and side dishes are a part of every menu on land or sea. Author's collection.*

Vegetables & Side Dishes

Prime rib and ...? Leg of lamb with ...? *Huevos con* ...? *Schnitzel mit* ...? Every main course has to have one and preferably two side dishes to accompany it. However good the entrée, it will be even better with an accompaniment of carrots, peas, rice, potatoes, tomatoes, creamed onions or any of a hundred other things. In addition to helping round out a well-balanced meal, side dishes punctuate the main course. In a type of culinary yin and yang, what is served along with the featured dish makes it taste better, either by complementing its flavor or as a contrast.

Although we often try to include the unusual with our dinners, we sometimes surprise our guests with something simple. Carrots, potatoes and peas almost stand on their own. But, as you're about to see, sometimes we can't help adding a little something extra ... or two somethings ... or three somethings ...

While our guests dine in the officers' saloon, the galley crew enjoys the same meal (between serving the courses) in the crew mess. Left to right, Aldred Chipman, Jason Jaffee, Wes Masterson, Diana Jaffee, Author. Photo: Bev Masterson.

Artichokes Vinaigrette

This dish is a pleasant departure from the normal way of serving artichokes, hot from the stove. We offered this as part of our *Creole Queen* dinner on "New Orleans Night." It comes from the bayous of Louisiana, but I imagine Castroville, California, which calls itself "The Artichoke Capital of the World" is familiar with it, too.

You might consider this a salad, because it's served cold, rather than a vegetable dish. In any case, it is best presented as a separate course, with extra bowls to throw the artichoke leaves in. An interesting serving variation is to offer it after the main course, in the European style.

Directions

Trim the stems off the artichokes with a sharp knife. Snip off the pointed ends of the leaves with scissors. Holding each one firmly with one hand, pound them upside down on a flat surface to open them. Rinse under cold running water and shake to remove most of the moisture. Place the artichokes stem side down, side by side, in a heavy pot large enough to hold them. Add one inch of cold water, sprinkle with the salt and the

Ingredients

4 medium or large fresh artichokes
Cold water
1 tsp. salt
½ tsp. finely minced garlic
1 ½ C. vinaigrette dressing

Vinaigrette dressing

1 ½ C. extra virgin olive oil
6 TBS. rice wine vinegar
6 TBS. lemon juice
3 tsp. freshly minced garlic
3/4 tsp. salt
1½ tsp. freshly ground white pepper
3/8 tsp. dry mustard
1 tsp. minced fresh parsley

NOTE:
With artichokes it's important not to use too much water, about one inch will do, and don't overcook them.

Artichokes steaming in the big kettle on the O'Brien*'s coal-fired stove. Photo: S. Rose.*

garlic. Turn the heat to high and bring the water to a boil. Cover and reduce heat to low, cooking for about forty-five minutes. Remove immediately from the water and drain upside down. Allow to cool to room temperature, place on a platter, cover with plastic wrap and refrigerate until ready to serve.

Meanwhile, mix all the ingredients for the vinaigrette dressing in a small bowl and let it sit, covered for about one hour.

Serve each artichoke on a plate with the dressing in a small glass bowl for dipping.

Serves 4.

Baked Potatoes á là O'Brien

This is not the traditional "Potatoes O'Brien" one finds in cookbooks, but an innovative variation on pan baked potatoes provided by our chief steward, Jim Hallstrom. Naturally, since it was created and served on the ship, it took our ship's name.

Directions

Parboil the potato wedges for about five minutes. Mix the butter, onion and spices in a large bowl. Add the potatoes and toss to coat. Place on a cookie sheet, cover with foil and bake at 350°F. for twenty-five minutes or until done. Remove foil and cook ten more minutes if "crust" is desired.

Serves 8-12.

Ingredients

10-12 russet potatoes, washed and cut in wedges but not peeled
1 lb. melted butter
1 tsp. paprika
1 tsp. garlic powder
1 tsp. salt and pepper
1 large yellow onion, grated

The annual cruises in May and October are times when the crew sleeps on board the O'Brien. Here Chief Steward Jim Hallstrom fries eggs for Saturday morning breakfast before the first cruise of San Francisco's Fleet Week in October, 2000. Photo: author.

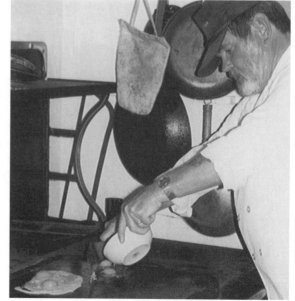

Carrots O'Brien

Ingredients

2 lb. carrots
water
¼ C. unsalted butter
3 TBS. dark brown
 sugar
¼ C. Drambuie
1 tsp. dried dill weed or
 1 TBS. chopped fresh
 dill weed.

NOTES:
1. The peeled baby
carrots you get at the
market are handy for
this. They're bite-sized
and don't need peeling
or slicing. Also, the
flavor is a little better
than mature carrots.
2. If you use the stan-
dard carrot, peel it and
slice it in ¼-inch slices.
Slice the carrot at an
angle and the slices will
be oblong and less likely
to roll away from you.
3. You can substitute
any liqueur, depending
on the mood you're in
and the effect you want
— Amaretto, Cointreau,
kirschwasser, etc.

This is my own creation, and of course
it was named after the ship. We served
this as part of one of our *Monterey*
dinners. Two of our guests (out of eight,
and that ain't bad) said they normally
don't eat carrots but, after trying these,
they finished what they had and asked for
seconds.

Directions

*In a medium pot with enough water
to cover, boil carrots, covered, until
cooked. When the carrots are done, drain
them in a colander, return to pot, add
butter, sugar and liqueur. Cover and let
steep for about ten minutes, shaking the
pot two or three times. Add dill, shake
again and serve.*

Serves 8.

*The Drambuie Liqueur Com-
pany Ltd.*

Lemon Rice Pilaf

What makes a rice dish a "pilaf" is that it's cooked in broth instead of water. It's that simple. We served this dish as part of a dinner from a menu that came from the passenger liner, *Mariposa*. The lemon gives it a little piquancy which makes it a good accompaniment to chicken or fish.

Directions

Sauté the onion in the butter with the cumin seeds uncovered in a medium-sized pot over medium heat until soft, about five minutes. Add the broth, rice, lemon, a sprinkle of salt and increase heat to high. When the mixture comes to a rolling boil, reduce heat to low, cover and cook ten minutes. Remove from heat and let sit, covered, for ten minutes. Uncover, fluff with a fork and serve. Sprinkle with toasted almonds.

Serves 6-8.

Ingredients

1 C. rice
1 ½ C. chicken broth
1 medium onion,
 chopped
grated rind of 1 lemon
1 TBS. butter
1 tsp. cumin seeds
salt
¼ C. slivered almonds,
 toasted

NOTE:
Whether you use short, medium or long grain rice is really a matter of personal preference. The short grain tends to be a little stickier; the long grain is drier and fluffs up more.

Oakland Collard Greens

Ingredients

2 bunches collard
  greens, chopped
  medium
2 large white onions,
  chopped medium
3 cloves garlic, minced
  fine
¼ lb. salt pork, minced
1 TBS. pepper
1 tsp. sugar
1 TBS. red pepper flakes
2 TBS. olive oil

NOTE:
1. For a variation, serve
with vinegar.
2. If collard greens are
unavailable, chard may
be substituted.

From time to time we have Navy cooks who volunteer to man the galley for our ship's crew's meals. This recipe came from a tin can (destroyer) sailor, and according to Rich Vannucci it is "one of our crew's very favorite vegetables."

Directions

Bring greens to boil over high heat, reduce heat to medium-low and simmer for one hour or until tender. Meanwhile, in a frying pan, over medium low heat, slowly sauté onions, garlic, pork, sugar and pepper in olive oil. Put onion mix aside. Remove greens and drain. Return greens to frying pan, add onion mix and combine well. Simmer for twenty minutes. Just before serving, add red pepper flakes.

Serves 8.

The destroyer Kidd *as she appeared in 1945 at the Hunter's Point Naval Shipyard. Photo: U.S. Navy.*

Pan-fried Potatoes

James Beard said, "I can't imagine civilization without the onion." That's quite a statement, but the more cooking one does the more one realizes the truth behind it. A close second in the necessities of civilization is the potato. Fried, boiled, baked, there are so many things that can be done with a good potato. Pan-frying is a favorite. Start with the basic recipe, then try the variations, or work up your own variation. It's difficult to go wrong when you fry potatoes.

Directions

Heat olive oil and butter in a large skillet over medium heat until butter is melted. Add onion, potatoes, half the garlic, salt and pepper. Cook, stirring occasionally, for about fifteen minutes or until potatoes are golden brown. Stir in remaining garlic, cook for one minute and serve.

Variations:

#1, Zesty Potatoes.

For a Mexican style dish, add the following ingredients to the basic recipe at the same time as the potatoes.
1 Anaheim or Jalapeno pepper, seeds removed, chopped

Ingredients

4 medium russet pota-
   toes, diced or sliced
2 TBS. butter
2 TBS. olive oil
1 medium onion,
   chopped
2 cloves garlic, chopped
salt
pepper

NOTES:
1. If potatoes are diced, try ¼-inch pieces, if sliced, make them a bit thinner.
2. Use only half the garlic at the beginning because, although it enhances the flavor of the dish, the true garlic flavor gets lost in the cooking.

1 TBS. paprika
2 tsp. powdered cumin
1 tsp. chili powder
(For a breakfast dish with zing, mix Mexican chorizo sausage with above.)

#2, Potatoes Provençal

Substitute red-skinned potatoes for the russets in the basic recipe, add the following ingredients at the same time as the potatoes.
6 medium new (red-skinned) potatoes
1 TBS. chopped, fresh dill weed
1 tsp. caraway seeds
1 tsp. chopped fresh tarragon.

#3. Breakfast Potatoes.

Add the following to variation #2 at the same time as the potatoes.
4 Italian sausages or 8 link pork sausages, cut in pieces, or equivalent amount of sausage meat.

#4. Potatoes and mushrooms.

Add one of the following to the basic recipe.
1 portobello mushroom cut in ½-inch squares
1 C. white mushrooms cut in 1/8-inch slices.

Serves 6-8.

Pecan Wild Rice Dressing

This is a good accompaniment to any roast meat entrée such as leg of lamb, prime rib or pork. We served it as a side dish in our "Showboat" dinner and had guests asking for seconds and thirds. Be sure to toast the pecans beforehand. The flavor is memorable.

Directions

Combine everything except the pecans and orange slices in a pan and cook, covered, until the liquid boils down to the level of the rice. Reduce heat to low and cook for about forty-five minutes or until wild rice is done (the grains begin to split). Stir occasionally to prevent scorching. Just before serving, toss with pecans. Garnish with orange slices and serve.

Serves 8.

Ingredients

1 C. long-grain white rice
½ C. wild rice
Chicken broth to cover rice by one inch
1 TBS. olive oil
1 TBS. grated orange rind
¼ C. orange juice
salt and pepper to taste
1 tsp. minced fresh garlic
¼ C. minced parsley
½ C. toasted pecans, chopped (chop before toasting)
Orange slices for garnish

Sicilian Spinach Fritters

Ingredients

10 oz. package frozen
   spinach, cooked and
   drained
¼ C. Parmesan cheese,
   grated
2 eggs, well beaten
1 C. milk
1 clove garlic, chopped
   fine
salt and pepper to taste
1 C. Bisquick or 1 C.
   flour with 1 TBS.
   baking powder
¼ C. olive oil

Joe Guzzetta, who made part of our Normandy trip in 1994, is, as you might guess, Italian. Do Italians make the best cooks? Well, among the cooks on the *Jeremiah O'Brien* are Joe Guzzetta, Rich Vannucci and Ed Lodigiani. The names say it all. And their recipes prove the point. According to Joe this recipe is *"molto bene."*

Directions

Heat oil in a frying pan over medium high heat. Beat all ingredients together to form a smooth batter. Spoon batter in tablespoon-sized portions into hot oil. Fry to golden brown on both sides. Drain on paper towels.

Serves 6

The O'Brien's five-month voyage to Normandy in 1994 required stores to last a long time. Left, canned goods and vegetables on deck before being taken below; right, potatoes stowed on the boat deck. Photos: author.

Smothered Okra

Of course, Cajun country is Louisiana which is New Orleans which is Bourbon Street. Photo: New Orleans Tourist Bureau.

Okra takes a bad rap. In a recent survey in *Bon Appetit* magazine it was voted one of the least liked of all vegetables. The problem is most people simply serve it plain. It's one of those vegetables that by itself is boring, but when cooked with the right combination of other vegetables and spices comes into its own as a great dish. This recipe comes from Cajun country and is one we used on our *Creole Queen* raffle prize dinner.

Directions

In a heavy four to five quart pan, melt the lard over medium heat. Sauté the onion until light brown (about fifteen minutes), stirring frequently. Add the sliced okra and sauté for fifteen minutes more, gradually adding the salt, pepper, cayenne, mace, sugar and chili powder. Add the drained tomatoes and the thyme and continue to sauté. Break up the tomatoes as the mixture cooks. Add the mustard. Cover and cook over low heat for another thirty minutes, stirring from time to time.

Serves 4.

Ingredients

3 TBS. lard
2 C. thinly sliced onion (two medium onions should do)
2 lb. fresh okra, stems and tips removed, cut crosswise in ½-inch slices
1½ tsp. salt
½ tsp. black pepper
1/8 tsp. cayenne
½ tsp. mace
¼ tsp. sugar
¼ tsp. chili powder
1-lb. can whole peeled tomatoes, drained
¼ tsp. dried thyme
2 tsp. Dijon mustard

Spanish Wild Rice

Ingredients

1 C. wild rice
4 C. chicken broth
1 medium onion,
    chopped
1 Anaheim pepper,
    seeded and chopped
1-lb. can chopped toma-
    toes, drained
¼ C. bacon drippings
1 TBS. chili powder
1 tsp. salt
1 tsp. sugar
½ C. grated Monterey
    Jack cheese

Wild rice is a mainstay of Minnesota cooking where much of it is grown. In recent years it has been grown in California with some success. Not everyone likes it, but for those that do, its rich, slightly nutty flavor enhances any meal. We served it on the *O'Brien* on one of our *President Cleveland* dinners and it made a nice counterpoint to the main course. By the way, the dish is even better when reheated the second day, after the flavors have had time to blend.

Directions

Soak the rice in hot tap water for thirty minutes, drain. Place in a three-quart pan and add chicken broth. Bring to a slow boil, reduce heat to a simmer and cook covered for forty-five minutes. Turn off heat and let sit for fifteen minutes.

In a second pan sauté the onion and pepper in the bacon drippings for about five minutes or until tender. Add the tomatoes to warm them through. Add the chili powder, sugar and salt. Pour off excess liquid from rice, add vegetables and blend. Top with grated cheese.

Serves 6.

Spring Peas in Thyme

Peas are a favorite side dish in our O'Brien dinners. They're attractive, tasty and their bright green color sets off just about any dish you serve them with. While frozen peas are almost as good as fresh (there's a trade off between the labor involved in shucking fresh peas and their succulent, sweet flavor) canned peas are another taste entirely. There's nothing wrong with canned peas, but I always consider them a different vegetable from fresh or frozen, simply because the flavor is so, well, canned.

Directions

Melt the butter in a saucepan and add the peas. Sprinkle lightly with salt and shake until the peas are covered with the butter. Add the hot water, cover and cook for about ten minutes or until tender. Add the thyme just before serving.

Serves 6-8.

Ingredients

2 lbs. shelled peas
2 TBS. butter
2 TBS. hot water
1 tsp. thyme
salt

NOTE:
Of course, fresh thyme works better than dried, giving a fresher, cleaner flavor. You can also vary the flavor by substituting oregano, basil, mint or just about any other herb.

Strike-me-blind

Ingredients

2 oz. salt pork, diced
1 C. rice
1½ C. water

This dish is basically rice with a bit of salt pork added. In fact the original recipe was "fatpork embedded in half a kidful of boiled and sticky rice." It originated in the ships in the Calcutta trade of the early and mid-1800s. The name came about because it was said the chickens carried on those ships became blind from eating rice and nothing else. Of course, rice was plentiful in India and the Orient, where most of these ships traded. Although ridiculously simple, the recipe is included in the interest of keeping the old traditions alive. If you'd like a rice side dish with a bit of variation, it's worth a try — but, of course, not as a steady diet.

Directions

Place ingredients in a medium saucepan over high heat. Once the water comes to a rolling boil, reduce heat to low and cover. After ten minutes, remove from heat, fluff rice with a fork, cover and let rest for ten minutes.

Serves 4.

Breadmaking is very much a hands-on process. We might use an electric mixer initially, but the actual kneading and forming of loaves is done the old-fashioned way. Above, left, Aldred Chipman mixing buttermilk biscuits; above, right, Chipman kneading the dough for "Those Short French Bastards." (p. 150); below left, Darcy Chipman kneading dough for French bread; below, right, one day's baking on the Jeremiah O'Brien's Normandy voyage. Photos: upper left and right, S. Rose, lower left, author, lower right, Bruce McMurtry.*

Breads, Rolls and Biscuits

Darcy Chipman forms the loaf, the last step before baking. Photo: author.

Hot from the oven, slathered with butter, fresh bread can be a meal in itself. Of course we don't do that too often, or our calorie intake might jump off the chart. But once in a while it sure is good.

Breadmaking is truly an art. Getting that near-perfect combination of inner texture, the outer crust, pleasing appearance and heavenly aroma takes practice. It's especially challenging on a coal-fired stove where the temperature is random and the oven just loves to turn crusts black. We've probably had more problems baking bread and rolls than anything else, but that, too, is part of the fun.

In the pages that follow you'll find some of our favorites. We left out the standard recipes that you find in every cookbook, you already know how to do those. These are a little different, and oh, so good.

Aberdeen Butteries

We needed a bread to complement our *Inchcliffe Castle* menu. The canon of Glencannon stories doesn't mention bread or rolls, but figuring that whatever kind of bread they had would certainly originate somewhere in the United Kingdom, I came up with a variation on this recipe from a Scottish cookbook called *A Feast of Scotland*. These rolls are said to originate from the French croissant, but although they taste similar, the shape and texture are entirely different. Supposedly they come from the Aberdeen fishing fleets where the high butter content kept the fishermen warm in the icy northern seas.

Directions

Dissolve the sugar in the water, add the yeast, mix and allow to proof. Put the flour in a large mixing bowl, add the liquid and mix to form a dough. Turn onto a floured surface and knead the dough until it is smooth. Place in a buttered bowl, cover with plastic wrap, and let rise for about forty-five minutes or until doubled in bulk. Punch the dough down. Beat the butter and lard together and divide them into three equal portions. Roll the dough out into an

Ingredients

4 C. flour
1 pkg. yeast
1 tsp. sugar
1 C. butter at room temperature
½ C. lard at room temperature
1¼ C. lukewarm water

Colin St. Andrew MacThrockle Glencannon, chief engineer of the SS Inchcliffe Castle.

Scottish fishing vessels at low tide in the harbor of Gourdon, Kincardine. Photo: Scottish Field.

oblong shape and dot the top two-thirds with one portion of the butter mix. Fold the bottom third up over the middle third and the top third down over the other two thirds and seal the edges. Let rest in a cool place for about thirty minutes and repeat the process twice more, giving the dough a quarter turn each time and allowing it to rest after each rolling. Divide the dough into eighteen ovals and place them on buttered baking trays, spacing them to allow for expansion. Let rest for thirty minutes, then bake for about twenty-five minutes at 400°F. until golden brown.

Makes 18 rolls.

These were so good, the crew took the leftovers home with them.

Buttermilk Biscuits

When it comes to buttermilk as a drink, most people can take it or leave it. But as a flavoring, it is one of the most versatile and savory enhancements imaginable. You can use it in salad dressings, pancakes, waffles, curries, dips, pies, cakes — the variations are endless. One of the best places for buttermilk is in biscuits. We served buttermilk biscuits in our "Showboat" dinner and they quickly disappeared.

Directions

Sift the flour, salt, baking powder and baking soda together. Cut in the Crisco. Pour in the buttermilk and mix with a fork. Gather the dough into a ball and place on a floured surface. Knead seven times, roll out to ½-inch thickness. Cut into desired shapes and bake on an ungreased cookie sheet for ten minutes at 450°F.

Makes about 2 dozen.

Ingredients

2 C. flour
3/4 tsp. salt
2 tsp. baking powder
½ tsp. baking soda
5 TBS. Crisco shortning
1 C. buttermilk

NOTE:
Use a cookie cutter or juice glass with the rim floured to cut into perfect rounds.

The paddle-wheel steamer Delta King *"comin' 'round the bend" in the San Joaquin River in the late 1930s. Photo: The Bank of Stockton.*

Cornbread

Ingredients

1 C. yellow corn meal
1 C. flour
1 TBS. sugar
4 tsp. baking powder
1 tsp. salt
1/8 tsp. allspice
1/8 tsp. freshly ground
   white pepper
1 large egg
1 C. milk
¼ C. vegetable oil
1½ TBS. bacon drip-
   pings

NOTES:
1. **Bacon drippings are essential. The flavor they give the bread is a critical part of this dish. Put the bacon drippings in the cast iron skillet, place in the oven until it melts, then pour in the batter.**
2. **For a crisp crust, put a pie-pan two-thirds full of water on the rack under the one the cornbread goes on before you preheat the oven.**
3. **For some "crunch" in the texture, add the kernels from an ear of fresh white corn.**

Cornbread is one of those dishes that invites controversy. There are Northern recipes (usually with more sugar) and Southern recipes (with less sugar). Some cooks insist on baking it in a skillet, others add a lot of peppers, whole corn and other things. Like most cooking, whatever recipe you like is the one that is best. Experiment a little and come up with your own version.

We served this for our *Creole Queen* raffle prize dinner. Its roots are along the Mississippi and it is a favorite on the *O'Brien.*

Directions

Preheat oven to 425°F. Stir the dry ingredients together in a large mixing bowl. Add the egg, milk and ¼ C. of shortening and beat with a wooden spoon until smooth. Grease an 8- or 9-inch cast iron skillet with the bacon drippings. Pour in the batter and bake for twenty-five to thirty minutes or until light golden brown on top. Cut the bread in wedges and serve in the skillet.

Serves 8-10.

Dinner Rolls

This is a recipe that suffered, not because of the *O'Brien's* coal-fired stove itself, but from the environment we were working in. Our problem was that the galley gets so hot it's difficult to find a place for a yeast dough to rise properly. The logical thing is to raise the dough in another room. But a ship tied up at Fisherman's Wharf in San Francisco without the engines operating doesn't have a lot of warm places on it. San Francisco weather is rarely freezing, but it can be pretty darn cold. And this time the cold wind whistled through the passageways chilling everything except the galley. Too hot or too cold. What to do? We killed the yeast again.

But don't worry. You can make these at home without a problem. They're a soft, tasty, slightly sweet variation on the classic Parker House Roll.

Ingredients

2 pkg. active dry yeast
2 TBS. granulated sugar
½ C. warm water (approx. 100°F. to 115°F.)
½ stick (¼ C.) butter, cut into small pieces
2 C. warm milk
5 to 6 C. all-purpose flour
2 tsp. salt
¼ to ½ C. melted butter
1 egg, beaten with 2 TBS. milk

Directions

Dissolve the yeast and the sugar in the warm water and allow to proof. Melt the ½ stick butter in the warm milk, then combine with the yeast in a large mixing bowl. Combine 2 to 3 C. of flour with the salt and stir into the mixture in the bowl, beating vigorously with a wooden spoon

The shelf above the stove is a favorite place to keep dishes warm (next to the syrup bottle in this photo) but is often too hot for dough to raise. Photo: author.

Kneading dough with your bare hands is one of the more Zen-like aspects of breadmaking. You come away with dry, clean flour on your fingers and a genuine sense of accomplishment. Photo: S. Rose.

Things don't always come out the way we planned. We forgot these for a couple of minutes and the coal heat made short work of them. Luckily, we had a better batch which we served to the guests. The galley crew cut off the burned parts and enjoyed the rest. Photo: S. Rose.

to make a soft sponge. This will produce a wet, sticky dough. Cover the bowl with plastic wrap, set in a warm place (not anywhere near a coal-fired stove) and let the dough rise until it doubles in bulk, about 1 hour. Stir down with a wooden spoon and add 2 more C. of flour, to make a dough that can be kneaded easily. Turn out on a lightly floured board and knead until smooth and elastic. Let the dough rest for a few minutes, then form it into a ball. Put the dough into a buttered bowl and turn to coat the surface thoroughly with butter. Cover and put in a warm, draft-free place to rise again until doubled in bulk, about an hour.

Punch down the dough, turn out on a lightly floured board and let rest for several minutes. Roll it out to a thickness of ½ inch. Break off walnut sized pieces of dough. Roll each piece into a ball. Dip in melted butter and place in groups of three in a muffin tin. Allow to rise again. Brush with the egg wash, and bake in a preheated 375°F. oven until lightly browned, about twenty minutes.

Serve piping hot with plenty of butter and honey or your favorite jam or marmalade.

Makes 30 rolls.

Evil Biscuits

The Monterey *ran from San Francisco to the South Pacific in the 1950s and 1960s.* Photo: Matson Lines.

They're called evil because they're so diabolically good you can't stop eating them. No matter how many you make, there's never enough. The first time we served them we made one batch and they vanished instantly. The next time we doubled the recipe — same result. When we served them as part of a dinner based on a menu from the liner *Monterey*, we couldn't make them fast enough. Last Thanksgiving, at home, we were up to quadrupling or quintupling the recipe, and they still disappeared. Whether it's the cream or the butter or both that makes them so outrageously tasty, this is a guaranteed hit.

Ingredients

2 C. all-purpose flour
1 tsp. salt
1 TBS. double acting
   baking powder
2 tsp. sugar
1 C. whipping cream
¼ lb. melted butter

Directions

Combine the dry ingredients and add the cream, mixing until a soft dough is formed. Turn out onto a floured board and knead for about a minute. Pat or roll to a thickness of about ½ inch. Cut in rounds or squares, dip in melted butter and arrange on a buttered baking sheet. Bake in a preheated 425°F. oven for about fifteen minutes, or until slightly brown. Serve very hot.

Makes 12 biscuits.

NOTE:
1. To cut in circles, flour the rim of a drinking glass and use it as your cutter.
2. Alternatively, cutting in squares yields wonderful crispy corners and edges.

Irish Soda Bread

Ingredients

3 C. whole-wheat flour
1 C. white flour
1 TBS. salt
1 tsp. baking soda
3/4 tsp. double-acting
   baking powder
2 C. buttermilk

We served this bread in one of our early dinners on the *Jeremiah O'Brien* and our guests seemed to enjoy it. According to tradition, Irish soda bread should be baked over a peat fire in a three-legged iron pot. It seemed a logical choice for our coal-fired stove which, if you think about it, is a lot closer to being a peat fire than the range at home. James Beard recommends it be served, sliced thin and buttered, for breakfast or tea. I think it would be a natural with a corned beef and cabbage dinner.

Directions

Mix the dry ingredients, then add enough buttermilk to make a soft dough, similar to a biscuit dough, but firm enough to hold its shape. Knead on a lightly floured board for three minutes, until smooth and velvety. Form into a round loaf and place on a well-buttered cookie sheet. Cut a cross all the way across the top of the loaf with a sharp, floured knife. Bake in a preheated 375°F. oven for about forty minutes or until the loaf is brown and sounds hollow when rapped with the knuckles.

Makes 1 large loaf.

Orange Nut Bread

This is an extremely popular bread in our house. My wife is fond of oranges and this was an instant hit. Starting with one of James Beard's recipes for banana bread, I experimented, and, after a few changes and failed attempts, came up with something that brings out the character of the orange and yet is a light bread, without that cake-like heaviness you so often find in banana bread.

Directions

Combine the flour with the soda and salt. Cream the butter and gradually add the sugar. Add the flour mixture, eggs, orange juice and milk. Mix well. Stir in the orange rind and nuts. Pour into a well-buttered 9x5x3 pan. Bake in a pre-heated 350°F oven for one hour or until a toothpick inserted in the center comes out dry.

Makes 1 loaf.

Ingredients

3 C. flour
1 tsp. baking soda
½ tsp. salt
½ C. butter at room
  temperature
1 C. sugar
2 eggs
1 C. orange juice
1/3 C. milk
grated rind of one
  orange
½ C. chopped toasted
  walnuts or pecans

Peanut Butter Banana Nut Bread

Yes, that's right. Peanut butter. It goes great with bananas. Here's a way to mix the flavors yet, rather than a heavy and filling sandwich, enjoy them in a slice of light bread. This was another experiment based on banana bread. It is surprisingly pleasant tasting.

Ingredients

¼ C. butter at room temperature
½ C. sugar
½ C. dark Karo syrup
2 eggs
1½ C. mashed, ripe bananas (about three)
1½ C. flour
½ C. smooth peanut butter
½ tsp. baking soda
½ tsp salt
½ C. toasted, chopped nuts, almonds or pecans

Directions

Cream the butter. Add the sugar and syrup and beat until creamy. Add the eggs, bananas, flour, peanut butter, baking soda and salt. Mix well. Fold in the nuts. Pour into a well-buttered 9x5x3 pan and bake in a pre-heated oven at 350°F. for one hour or until a toothpick inserted in the center comes out clean.

Makes 1 loaf.

Those Short French Bastards

This is an example of something that turned out terrific despite several well-intended deviations from the original recipe that should have made a total mess of it.

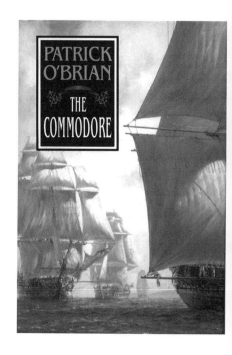

One of the raffle prize dinners we did on the SS *Jeremiah O'Brien* was based on the Aubrey/Maturin novels of Patrick O'Brian. This series is a favorite with seafarers, ranking right up there with Forrester's Hornblower series. When the companion cookbook for the Patrick O'Brian novels, *Lobscouse and Spotted Dog,* came out it seemed a natural for the nautical diners we featured on board, with adjustments for our temperamental stove, of course.

According to the authors, the "Bastard" in question was a loaf of French bread referred to as *pain bâtard* which was common at the time (late 1700s-early 1800s). It is shorter and thicker than the standard baguette and with a bit of literary license, was translated in the novels to "The Last of the True French Short Bastards." Because the authors don't give a recipe ("period sources for such breads are impossible to find") I selected one from other sources called French-Style Bread.

Ingredients

1½ pkg. active dry
   yeast
1 TBS. granulated sugar
2 C. warm water
   (100°F. to 115°F.
   approximately)
1 TBS. salt
5 to 6 C. all purpose or
   hard-wheat flour
3 TBS. yellow cornmeal
1 TBS. egg white, mixed
   with 1 TBS. cold water

Directions

Combine the yeast with sugar and warm water in a large bowl and allow to proof. Combine the salt with the flour and add to the yeast mixture, a cup at a time, until you have a stiff dough. Remove to a lightly floured board and knead until no longer sticky, about ten minutes, adding flour as necessary. Place in a buttered bowl and turn to coat the surface with butter. Cover and let rise in a warm place until doubled in bulk, 1½ to 2 hours.

Punch down the dough. Turn out on a floured board and shape into two long, French bread-style loaves. Place on a baking sheet that has been sprinkled with the cornmeal but not buttered. Slash the tops of the loaves diagonally in two or three places, and brush with the egg wash. Place in a cold oven, set the temperature at 400°F., and bake 35 minutes, or until well browned and hollow sounding when the tops are rapped.

Makes 2 standard loaves (or 4 short ones).

Disasters and calamities are all part of the cooking experience. When you're

Our raffle prize dinners start with a clean work area, left, which is quickly filled, right. Photos: S. Rose.

working with a temperamental, unregulated coal stove, the possibilities multiply.

The night we made this on the ship it
seemed that everything went wrong
although our variations seemed logical.
First, we thought one package of yeast
didn't seem enough; two might be better.
Second, we substituted malt powder for
the sugar. Normally, this gives bread a
much finer texture. Third, we were very
busy so to save time, we mixed everything
in a power mixer and that was the real
beginning of our troubles. The dough
formed nicely and we added flour until it
no longer stuck to the bowl. But then it
formed one big lump on the beater and
simply turned around without actually
mixing. Busy with other dishes, we put
the dough in a buttered bowl, covered it
with plastic wrap and set it on a shelf
above the stove to rise. And rise it did. It
was three times its original size within an
hour. Because the bread should come
fresh from the oven when served and two
hours were calculated for the first rising
we simply left it there.

After the two hours were up we took
the plastic wrap off, punched it down, and
immediately realized something was
wrong. It stuck to our hands! It was too
moist. But it was too late to start again, so

During preparation, the spice rack becomes our bulletin board with menus, reminders and notes hung at eye level for quick reference. Photos: S. Rose.

we *had* to continue. Bearing in mind we said *"Short* French Bastards" in our menu, we made four short loaves rather than the two long ones called for by the original recipe. The loaves *were* short — and *flat*! Covering them with plastic wrap again, we put them above the stove to rise for another half hour. They didn't rise at all! With only forty minutes to dinner we had to continue. Whipping up a quick egg wash, we brushed the loaves, covered them with foil (coal cooking always burns the outside of bread and pastry if they're not covered) and put them in the oven hoping they might rise a bit. Half an hour later we removed the foil and returned them to the oven for a couple of minutes to brown the crusts. Soon they were done — and just as flat as ever. We sliced them crosswise in thin biscotti-shaped strips and served them in baskets. Tasting a piece we were surprised to find it had a crunchy crust, soft inside and tasted delicious. Our guests ate every last one and raved about them!

For any given dinner we usually have several dishes going at once: top, syrup warming; top right, a couple of items staying warm in foil; lower right, back, melted butter (note inverted pie tin to keep it from getting too hot); lower right, front, a sauce cooking; lower center, green peas simmering; lower left, an improvised double boiler (to melt chocolate); behind it, soup simmering. Photo: S. Rose.

That was our experience with "Those Short French Bastards." I don't know if we could ever duplicate the process, so many things went wrong. But sometimes we get lucky. This was one of those times.

White German Bread with Caraway Seeds

The second time we did *Breaded Veal Cutlet á là Holstein* it came from a 1968 menu of the SS *President Cleveland*, the American President Lines trans-Pacific passenger liner. Because the menu had a German basis, we added a good German bread, the kind they serve for breakfast in some of the working men's hotels in that country. In German it is called *Weissbrot mit Kümmel*, or "white bread with caraway." It's a good recipe, fairly simple and fun, because of the way you let the bread rise.

Ingredients

¼ C. lukewarm water
3 pkgs. dry yeast
2 tsp. sugar
½ C. lukewarm milk
4 C. all purpose flour
2 eggs at room temperature
¼ lb. unsalted butter, cut into pieces and softened to room temperature
1 TBS. salt
1 TBS. caraway seeds
corn meal

Directions

Pour the lukewarm water into a small mixing bowl and sprinkle the yeast and ½ tsp. sugar into it. Let stand for two to three minutes, stir together to dissolve, then set in a warm, draft-free place for three to five minutes or until double in volume.

Transfer to a large mixing bowl and stir in the milk with a wooden spoon. Beat in three cups of the flour about ¼ cup at a time. Beat in the eggs one at a time. Beat in the butter. Continue beating until the dough can be shaped into a compact ball.

Place the ball on a lightly floured board and knead in the remaining cup of

The SS President Cleveland *was in APL's Trans-Pacific service sailing from San Francisco with calls at Honolulu, Yokohama, Hong Kong and Manila every six weeks. Photo: American President Lines.*

NOTE:

Once we did this and the dough floated! Don't worry. Just rotate it occasionally and leave it in for the ten to fifteen minutes.

flour, a few tablespoons at a time. Knead until all the flour is added and the dough is stiff and dry. Shape into a rough ball, place in a mixing bowl and add enough cold water to cover it by several inches. In ten to fifteen minutes, the top of the dough should rise above the surface of the water.

Remove the dough from the water and pat the surface dry with paper towels. Return it to a floured board, punch it down, sprinkle with the remaining 1½ tsp. sugar, the salt and the caraway seeds. Knead for about ten minutes, adding flour as necessary, until the dough is smooth and elastic. Pat and shape the dough into a round loaf about eight inches in diameter.

Sprinkle a baking sheet lightly with cornmeal, place the dough in the center and cover loosely with a towel or plastic wrap. Let the dough rise in a warm, draft-free place for about thirty minutes, or until it doubles in bulk. Preheat the oven to 375°F.

Bake the bread in the middle of the oven for about one hour. The crust should be a light golden color.

Makes 1 loaf.

Apple Dumplings

Shrewsbury Cakes

Chocolate Ship Cookies

Spotted Dog with Custard Sauce

Zabaglione with Champagne and Raspberries

Deep Dish Apple Pie

Bananas Foster

French Vanilla Ice Cream

Dutch Almond Cake

Bread Pudding with Whiskey Sauce

Chess Pie

Joe Froggers

Chocolate Painted Eclairs with French Vanilla Cream

Fruit Cocktail Cake

Desserts

Dandyfunk

Key Lime Pie

Mocha Cake

Rhubarb Cobbler

No dining experience would be complete without a good dessert. To give our raffle prize winners an extra sense of elegance, we usually serve two. Cakes, pies, cookies, ice cream, cobblers, eclairs, puddings — at one time or another they have all made their way into the officers' saloon to finish off a good dinner. The challenge is to make them look so good that guests will taste them even if they are already stuffed, and to make them taste so good that they won't want to stop.

Usually we do the desserts early in the day. That way they are out of the way before we get into the time pressure of preparing and serving the various courses on schedule. Also, if the dessert doesn't turn out as expected, there's time to do it again if necessary. As you'll see, we — and our stove — have had a few disasters with desserts, but, in a way, that's part of the fun, too — how to recoup so that no one knows.

Charlotte de Russe

Ricotta Zeppole

French Silk Pie

Apple Dumplings

This is one of those dishes that takes a lot of practice to do right on a coal-fired stove. The first time we tried it the pastry came out blackened and the apples weren't done; the second time the apples were done but the pastry came out pale and anemic looking. The third time was the charm, as they say. But don't worry, this will work fine in your stove at home where you can control the temperature and the heat doesn't attack the pastry dough. The recipe is a variation on one served in Colonial Williamsburg. We served it as the finale to one of our *President Roosevelt* dinners.

Ingredients

Pastry crust
2 C. all-purpose flour
1 tsp. salt
2 tsp. sugar
2/3 C. butter
4-5 TBS. ice water

Dumplings
Pastry Crust
6 large, whole apples, peeled and cored
1½ C. sugar
1¼ tsp. cinnamon
¼ tsp. nutmeg
6 TBS. butter
2 C. hot water

Directions

For the pastry crust
Mix dry ingredients together. Blend in shortening with knives or pastry blender until mixture has the consistency of small gravel. Moisten with enough ice water to just hold the dough together. Form in a ball, cover with plastic wrap and chill for 1 hour.

For the dumplings
Preheat oven to 450°F. Roll out pastry to 1/8 inch thick and cut into six 8-

NOTES:
1. You can use Crisco or margarine instead of butter if you like, but the flavor won't be as good.
2. The thinner the pastry the better, but not so thin you can't work with it.
3. Use Macintosh or some other apple with a distinctive flavor.
4. Be sure the dumplings are not touching, so the pastry browns evenly.
5. Frequent basting is critical to the appearance of the dish. It ensures even browning and makes the pastry much more pleasing to the eye.

inch squares. Place an apple in the center of each square. Combine ½ C. sugar, ½ tsp. cinnamon, ¼ tsp. nutmeg and 2 TBS. butter. Divide between the apples, filling the center of each one with the mixture. Moisten the edges of the pastry with cold water and fold up around the apples, pressing the edges together to seal firmly. Prick the pastry in several places with a fork. Chill for one hour. Combine the remaining sugar, cinnamon, butter and 2 C. hot water and boil five minutes. Place apples in baking dish and bake at 450°F. for ten minutes. Reduce heat to 350°F., pour syrup over apples and bake thirty-five minutes, basting occasionally.

Makes 6.

The President Roosevelt's Starlight Lounge was a place for passengers to meet for cocktails on her around-the-world service in the 1960s. Photo: American President Lines.

Bananas Foster

Simple elegance is the phrase that comes to mind with this recipe. It is very easy to prepare, yet the presentation is flamingly dramatic and tastes out of this world. Bananas Foster is very popular in New Orleans, where I believe it originated. This was part of our *Creole Queen* raffle prize dinner. Our problem with this dish on the *Jeremiah O'Brien* was we didn't have any freezers operating the night of the dinner. I bought the ice cream early in the day and packed it in an ice chest with ice, hoping for the best. Fat chance! Suffice it to say the ice cream was verrry soft when we scooped it out. Our Bananas Foster came out a bit on the soupy side. But you won't have that problem at home. It's a classy dessert for any meal.

Ingredients

2 TBS. butter
3 TBS. brown sugar
½ tsp. cinnamon
2 ripe bananas sliced lengthwise
¼ C. banana liqueur
¼ C. rum
2 scoops vanilla ice cream

Directions

Melt the butter over low heat in a large skillet or crêpes pan. Add the sugar and the cinnamon and mix well. Put the bananas in the pan and sauté until they begin to soften. Pour in the banana liqueur and half the rum. Continue cooking over low heat. Heat the remainder of the rum in a small saucepan over high heat until it begins to boil. Quickly pour the rum into the skillet and ignite. Tip the pan with a circular motion to distribute and prolong the flame at the same time basting the bananas with the mix. When the flame dies, serve two slices of banana on each plate and top with a scoop of vanilla ice cream. Spoon the remaining sauce over the ice cream.

Serves 2.

While a student learning piloting on the Mississippi, Mark Twain's teacher explained the process of "learning" the river:

"My boy, you've got to know the shape of the river perfectly. It is all there is left to steer by on a very dark night. Everything else is blotted out and gone. But mind you, it hasn't the same shape in the night it has in the daytime."

"How on earth am I ever going to learn it, then?"

"How do you follow a hall at home in the dark? Because you know the shape of it. You can't see it."

"Do you mean to say that I've got to know all the million trifling variations of shape in the banks of this interminable river as well as I know the shape of the front hall at home?"

"On my honor, you've got to know them better than any man ever did know the shape of the halls in his own house ...

"You see, this has got to be learned; there isn't any getting around it ... you only learn the shape of the river; and you learn it with such absolute certainty that you can always steer by the shape that's in your head, and never mind the one that's before your eyes."

Mark Twain
Life on the Mississippi
(1874)

Bread Pudding with Whiskey Sauce

We served this in one of our earlier dinners on the *Jeremiah O'Brien*. It came from a 1930s menu off the *General Pershing* which was operated by States Steamship Company at the time. This is probably as close as American cooking comes to the steamed pudding so prevalent in British fare, especially that from the sailing ship era. In any case, bread pudding is an all-time hit. This one had our guests clamoring for seconds. Or was it just the whiskey sauce they were after?

Directions

For the pudding

Arrange the bread evenly in a well buttered baking pan, 13x9x2 inches. Warm the milk and melt the butter into it. In a large bowl whisk together the milk mixture, eggs and vanilla. Whisk in the sugar, cinnamon and nutmeg and pour over the bread. Add the raisins to the bread mixture, stirring to combine well and smooth the top of the pudding. Place in a larger pan of water so water comes about half way up the sides of the pudding pan. Bake in the middle of a preheated 325°F. oven for an hour and fifteen minutes or until the pudding is set and a knife comes out clean.

Ingredients

Pudding
12 C. day old French bread, crusts removed, cut into 3/4 inch cubes
6 large eggs
6-8 C. whole milk
1/3 C. vanilla
1½ C. brown sugar
3 TBS. cinnamon
3 tsp. nutmeg
1 C. raisins
1½ sticks (3/4 C.) unsalted butter, cut into pieces

Whiskey sauce
2 sticks (1 C.) unsalted butter, cut into pieces
1½ C. sugar
½ C. Scotch whiskey
2 large eggs, beaten lightly

S. S. "General Pershing"
John S. Smith Commanding

CAPTAIN'S DINNER

NOTE:
Caution! In making the whiskey sauce be sure the sugar mixture isn't too hot. Doing this on the *O'Brien*'s coal-fired stove when it was too hot resulted in a sauce that looked like egg flower soup! In other words, if it is too hot the eggs will solidify in glumps instead of mixing in. We had to quickly make up another batch.

The General Pershing *of States Steamship Co. as she appeared in San Francisco on Sept. 30, 1935. The Indian good luck symbol on the stack and menu, above, is often confused with the Nazi swastika, which points in the opposite direction. Photo: San Francisco Maritime National Historical Park.*

For the whiskey sauce
In a medium saucepan melt the butter over moderate heat, add the sugar and cook the mixture, stirring constantly for two minutes, or until it is bubbly. Remove the pan from the heat. Stir in the whiskey gradually and cook the mixture over low heat until the sugar is dissolved. Stir about ¼ C. of the mixture into the eggs and stir the egg mixture back into the sugar mixture. Stir the sauce over low heat for about ten seconds or until it is thickened and transfer to a serving bowl.

Serves 12.

Charlotte de Russe

We finished off our raffle prize dinner based on the Pacific Mail Line steamer *Acapulco's* 1875 menu with this classic dessert. It takes time, but it is a lot of fun to put together and, when done right, makes a dramatic presentation. You should try making Bavarian cream on a coal-fired stove! With little temperature regulation, it meant spending a lot of time lifting the cream off the stove, then putting it back again, off again, on again, and so on. On second thought, you shouldn't try it that way.

Ingredients

1 Charlotte mold or
    spring form pan
Enough lady fingers to
    line the mold
2 C. milk
½ C. almond paste
4 egg yolks
1 TBS. unflavored
    gelatin
½ C. cold water
1 tsp. vanilla
2 C. whipping cream

Directions

Put the gelatin in the water to soften. Meanwhile, combine the milk and the almond paste in a sauce pan and cook over low heat, stirring constantly until the cream is smooth. Stir the mixture slowly into four beaten egg yolks and cook over hot water (use a double boiler) stirring until the custard is hot and slightly thickened. Add the gelatin water mix, cooking and stirring until the gelatin is dissolved. Place the saucepan in a bowl of cracked ice and stir until it cools and begins to set. Beat the whipping cream in a chilled bowl until it stands in soft peaks. Stir the vanilla into

NOTES:

1. **We used a spring form cake pan for this the day we made it on the *Jeremiah O'Brien*. It works just as well and, unless you have a huge kitchen, you save investing in and finding a place to store a Charlotte mold you might only use a couple of times a year.**

2. **The quantity of lady fingers you use will depend on the size of your mold and how you cut them up.**

the custard, then fold in the whipped cream. Refrigerate while you assemble the cake.

Begin at the bottom of the mold by placing a round piece of lady finger in the center. Cover the bottom with lady fingers cut into triangles, placing them close together around the center piece so they radiate from it like the petals of a flower. Place split lady fingers upright and close together all around the inside wall. Fill the mold with Bavarian cream and refrigerate for at least two hours. Unmold on a round serving plate. Serve with whipped cream and a fruit sauce, such as lemon curd, if you like.

Serves 8

Pacific Mail Steamship Company's

STEAMSHIP

A C A P U L C O

Saturday Oct 2? 1875

PUDDINGS, PASTRY, &c.

Tapioca Pudding

Apple & Cranberry Pies / assorted Pastry

Charlotte de Ruse

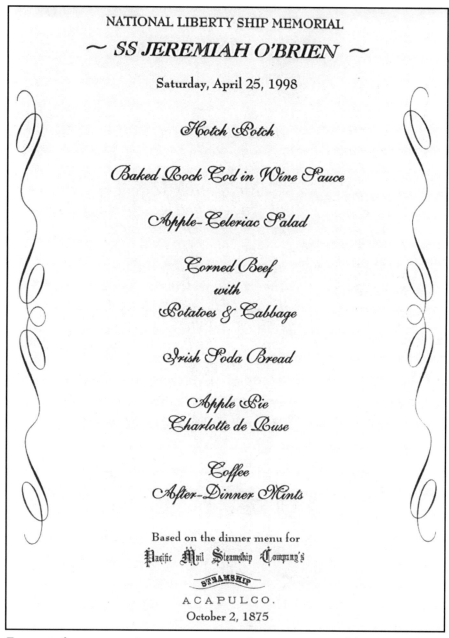

NATIONAL LIBERTY SHIP MEMORIAL

~ *SS JEREMIAH O'BRIEN* ~

Saturday, April 25, 1998

Hotch Potch

Baked Rock Cod in Wine Sauce

Apple-Celeriac Salad

Corned Beef
with
Potatoes & Cabbage

Irish Soda Bread

Apple Pie
Charlotte de Ruse

Coffee
After-Dinner Mints

Based on the dinner menu for
Pacific Mail Steamship Company's
STEAMSHIP
ACAPULCO.
October 2, 1875

For most of our presentation menus we try to adapt some aspect of the original. Here, the heading from the Acapulco's *menu was adapted to ours to give a sense of history and occasion.*

Time Capsule

After the Normandy Voyage

The following item about our stove appeared in the summer 1995 edition of *Steady As She Goes*, the ship's newsletter. Pat McCafferty is a veteran of the Normandy voyage and Anna Falche was chairman of the board at the time.

On May 21, 1995, Pat McCafferty brought bad news to Anna Falche. The O'Brien's 52 year old coal-fired stove had given up her last meal. It was time for a serious overhaul.

Earlier research had shown that the original manufacturer, Majestic Marine of St. Louis, Missouri, no longer made or repaired stoves.

Hoping for the best, Anna told Pat to strip down the stove, and that we would somehow find the money.

In the mail on Monday, May 22, came an unsolicited check for $5000.00 from a St. Louis, Missouri foundation.

That's the Lucky O'Brien for you.

There's more to this story. One of our raffle prize dinners was scheduled for a Saturday evening which, unknown to both Pat and us, was between the day he stripped down the stove and its planned reassembly. I arrived at noon with several bags of groceries and found the stove in pieces on the deck! What to do? Our guests were already en route from the northern part of the state. Working fast, everyone pitched in and put as much of it back together as we could, found a piece of expanded metal to use for a fire-box bed and cooked the dinner. The ship's "can-do" spirit came through again and our dinner guests didn't know the difference.

Chocolate Painted Éclairs with French Vanilla Cream

Dessert for our *Titanic* dinner was an attempt to recreate that served the first class passengers on the famous liner. Éclairs are a personal favorite; a sumptuous way to top off a good dinner. The pastry part of this recipe was a real challenge on the *O'Brien's* coal-fired stove with its fluctuating temperature and uneven oven heat that tends to burn the surface of breads, cakes and pastries. It should be much easier on your stove at home.

Directions

Pastry Cream

In a bowl, whisk together egg yolks and ¼ C. of the sugar for 2 minutes until pale yellow. Add flour in three additions, stir until mixed well.

In a saucepan, heat the milk, remaining sugar and vanilla bean over medium heat, stirring often for eight to ten minutes or until sugar is dissolved and small bubbles begin to form around the edges of the pot. Stirring constantly, pour about one-third of the milk mixture into the egg mixture and stir until thoroughly combined. Pour egg mixture into remaining milk and cook, stirring

Ingredients

Pastry Cream
6 egg yolks (at room temperature)
½ C. granulated sugar
5 TBS. all purpose flour
2 C. whole milk
1 vanilla bean, halved lengthwise
1 TBS. butter
½ C. whipping cream

Choux Pastry
1 C. water
½ C. butter
pinch of salt
1 ¼ C. all-purpose flour
5 eggs (at room temperature)
1 TBS. water
3 oz. bittersweet chocolate
powdered sugar

Whether it's eclairs, soup or anything else, the first step in the process is lighting off the range an hour before and getting it up to temperature. It begins with paper, cardboard, kindling and a few pieces of coal. Photo: S. Rose.

NOTES:

1. In making the pastry cream, if you add the flour all at once it won't make a bit of difference.
2. Resist the urge to substitute liquid vanilla for the bean. The real thing is so much more flavorful, and it makes the process a little more fun.
3. The plastic wrap prevents a film or crust from forming on top of the custard.

for two to three minutes or until mixture begins to mound and hold its shape; remove from heat. Stir in butter and remove vanilla bean. Transfer to bowl, cover with plastic wrap touching surface of the custard and cool to room temperature.

Beat whipping cream until stiff, add a large dollop of cream to cooled pastry cream and fold in; add remaining whipped cream and fold in until almost combined. Transfer to pastry bag fitted with ½-inch star tube. Place in refrigerator until completely chilled.

Choux Pastry
Meanwhile, in a heavy-bottomed saucepan set over high heat, bring water, butter and salt just to boil. Remove from heat and add flour all at once, stirring vigorously with a wooden spoon until mixture comes away from sides of pan, making a smooth ball.

Reduce heat to medium-low and cook flour mixture, stirring constantly for two minutes or until coating begins to form on bottom of pan. Turn into large bowl, stir for thirty seconds.

Make a well in the middle of the dough and, with an electric mixer, beat in

Once a good fire is going it requires frequent pampering. Photo: author.

Right, in the late afternoon, Bev and Wes Masterson get the tablecloths from the linen locker to begin setting the tables for dinner. Below, this is usually our guests' first view of where they are about to have dinner. Note the row of battle ribbons below the ship name above the lifeboat. Photos: right, S. Rose; bottom, author.

four of the eggs, one at a time, beating well after each addition. Continue beating until the mixture is smooth and shiny and holds its shape when lifted.

Place dough into piping bag fitted with 3/4 inch wide tip. On parchment-lined baking sheets, pipe fingers of dough about 4 inches long and 1 inch wide. In bowl, beat together remaining egg and 1 TBS. water, brush each bun lightly being careful not to drip down sides. Bake in 425°F. oven for twelve minutes; reduce heat to 375°F. and bake for five minutes longer or until golden brown. With a sharp knife, pierce each side of each éclair twice. Turn oven off and let éclairs stand for five minutes, then remove and cool on rack.

Melt chocolate over barely simmering water. Brush top of each cooled éclair with enough chocolate to coat well. Cool in refrigerator for five minutes to harden chocolate.

Cut éclairs in half lengthwise. Pull out any sticky dough in center, discard. Pipe pastry cream into bottom of each éclair. Replace chocolate-covered tops. Dust with powdered sugar just before serving.

Makes about two dozen.

NOTE:
Brushing the piped dough with egg wash before cooking takes a very delicate pastry brush to do properly.

Chess Pie

Ingredients

2 C. sugar
1 TBS. flour
¼ C. corn meal
¼ C. butter, softened
4 eggs beaten lightly
1 C. milk
¼ C. fresh lemon juice
¼ C. grated lemon rind
1 tsp. vanilla
1 deep-dish pie shell,
   uncooked

HINT:
The average lemon yields 2 tablespoons of juice.

This dessert started out as a simple pie, easily made with ingredients on hand on early farms. Through the years it has become a classic. The corn meal gives it a different texture and elevates it from being just another pie. We served this as a finish to our "Showboat" dinner along with "Downriver Chocolate Cake."

Directions

Combine sugar, flour and corn meal, mixing with a fork. Add the remaining ingredients. Stir until blended. Pour the filling in the pie shell. Bake in a 350°F. oven for about forty-five minutes. Cool before serving.

Serves 6-8.

One nice thing about cakes is, if necessary, you can cover a multitude of sins with the frosting. Here Aldred Chipman cuts the "Down River Chocolate Cake" into serving pieces. Photo: Bev Masterson.

Chocolate Ship Cookies

After she came out of the Suisun Bay Reserve Fleet in 1978 and was overhauled at Bethlehem Ship Yard in San Francisco, the *Jeremiah O'Brien*'s first berth was at Fort Mason. In those early years the volunteer crew did everything possible to raise money for the ship. In addition to charging admission and selling things from a small ship's store, they also sold food out of the galley on weekends. One item was hot dogs and the other was "Chocolate Ship Cookies." The original recipe left with one of the cooks many years ago, but this one is a good substitute.

Ingredients

1 C. butter
3/4 C. white sugar
3/4 C. brown sugar
1½ C. flour
1½ C. oatmeal
1 tsp. baking soda
2 eggs
1 TBS. vanilla
2/3 C. chocolate chips
1 C. toasted walnuts or
  pecans, chopped

Directions

Cream the butter and sugars together. Blend in the eggs and mix in the flour, oatmeal, baking soda and vanilla. Fold in chocolate chips and nuts. Drop tablespoon sized pieces of dough on a buttered baking sheet and cook at 350°F. for twelve to twenty minutes, depending on whether you want them soft or crunchy.

Makes 2 dozen cookies.

Dandyfunk

Ingredients

½ lb. hard tack, pounded
to a powder
water
¼ C. molasses or mar-
malade
¼ C. melted butter

This is another sailing ship recipe that's more of a dessert than anything else. Windjammer cooks had little to work with and had to be very creative when it came to making "something different."

Directions

Mix the powdered hard tack with enough water to form a paste. Blend in the melted butter and molasses or marmalade. Bake the resulting "cake" in a 350°F. oven for thirty minutes.

Serves 4.

Deep Dish Apple Pie

This is a classy variation on the traditional American favorite. Rich Vannucci grabbed it from the Navy volunteer cooks when he discovered how much the *O'Brien*'s crew enjoyed it.

Directions

Place apples in a 10x6x2 buttered baking dish. In a small bowl combine sugar and cinnamon, set aside 1 tsp. of the mixture. Mix cornstarch and salt with the remaining sugar mixture. Sprinkle evenly over the apples in the dish. In a medium bowl stir together the flour and nutmeg. Cut in the margarine until the mixture resembles coarse meal. Sprinkle 1 tsp. of the water over part of the mixture, gently tossing with a fork. Push to the side of the bowl. Repeat until all is moistened. Form into a ball. On a floured surface roll the dough into a 12x8 rectangle. Cut decorative vents in the pastry. Carefully place the pastry on top of the apples, fluting the edges to the side of the dish but not over the edge. Brush with milk and sprinkle with the reserved sugar mixture. Bake in a 375°F. oven for about forty minutes or until the apples are tender and the crust is golden brown.

Serves 8

Ingredients

6 C. apples, sliced, with skins on
½-2/3 C. sugar, depending on tartness of apples
1 tsp. cinnamon
1 TBS. cornstarch
1/8 tsp. salt
3/4 C. all purpose flour
¼ tsp. nutmeg
3 TBS. margarine
3 TBS. cold water
4 TBS. milk

NOTE:
The original recipe calls for peeled apples, but the skins add an extra dimension of flavor and texture, so I always leave them on.

Pictured below are apple pies from a different recipe, not deep dish, that we did for one of our raffle prize dinners. Photo: S. Rose.

Dutch Almond Cake

Ingredients

3/4 C. sugar
½ C. unsalted butter at
  room temperature
7-oz. pkg. almond
  paste, broken into
  pieces
3 large eggs at room
  temperature
1 TBS. kirsch or other
  cherry brandy
½ tsp. almond extract
¼ tsp. salt
1/3 C. cake flour
½ tsp. baking powder
½ C. slivered almonds,
  toasted
about 12 blanched,
  whole toasted al-
  monds
powdered sugar

NOTES:
1. Using toasted al-
monds in this recipe
gives an added taste
dimension to the cake.
Otherwise all the al-
mond flavors blend into
one.
2. By the way, you can
call it Italian Almond
Cake or Armenian or
Russian or whatever
nationality you would
like to highlight. No one
will know.
3. This cake has a nice,
dense texture due to the
small amount of flour
used. It's great as a
desert or for coffeetime.

One of our steamship menus listed this dessert which sounded interesting. But I couldn't find a "Dutch" almond cake anywhere. Probably the chef on that particular ship was from Holland and had his own recipe. We improvised and it came out very tasty, in spite of our usual problems with coal heat and sugar. In the end the cake had the right consistency, looked good and tasted great.

Directions

Preheat oven to 350°F. Butter an eight-inch diameter cake pan with 2-inch sides. Dust the pan with flour, tap out the excess. Using an electric mixer, beat sugar and butter in a large bowl until light and creamy. Add the almond paste, piece by piece, beating until blended after each addition. Beat in the eggs. Mix in the kirsch, almond extract and salt. Mix in the flour and baking powder until just blended. Fold in toasted almonds. Spoon the batter into the pan, smooth the top. Top with whole toasted almonds. Bake until cake top is golden brown and tester inserted into the center comes out clean. Cool in the pan on a rack. Transfer the cake to a platter, dust with powdered sugar and serve.

Serves 10-12.

French Silk Pie

PACIFIC COAST STEAMSHIP COMPANY

DINNER

Coastal steamers, while good feeders, were not known for the elegance of their cuisine. You can imagine my surprise when I found this dessert listed in the 1901 menu of a Pacific Coast Steamship Co. vessel. It was one of two desserts we served in one of the early raffle prize dinners. It's a nice recipe because it's relatively easy and the crust is unusual enough to make it interesting. You get an extra little unexpected crunch when eating this pie, a pleasant surprise.

Directions

Line the bottom and sides of an eight-inch pie plate with the coconut and bake at 250°F. for one hour or until golden. Transfer to a rack and let cool. In the top of a double boiler set over hot water, melt the chocolate with the brandy and coffee powder. In a bowl cream together the butter and sugar. Beat in the eggs one at a time, followed by the chocolate mixture and the nuts. Transfer to the pie shell and chill for at least 3 hours.

Serves 6-8.

Ingredients

1¼ C. sweetened, shredded coconut

2 oz. unsweetened chocolate

2 TBS. brandy

2 TBS. instant coffee powder

2 sticks butter, at room temperature

1 C. sugar

2 large eggs

½ C. toasted ground hazelnuts

½ C. toasted ground blanched almonds

NOTE:
Once again, the importance of toasting the nuts can't be overemphasized. Spread them on a cookie sheet in a 350°F. oven until golden.

Fruit Cocktail Cake

This is an interesting and very tasty recipe for an unusual cake. Rich Vannucci got it from one of the Navy cooks who frequently volunteer to cook on the *Jeremiah O'Brien* for the ship's crew. It looks festive, tastes great and is *very* rich.

Ingredients

For the cake
1½ C. flour
1½ C. sugar
1 tsp. cinnamon
1 tsp. baking soda
2 eggs, beaten
14-16 oz. can fruit cocktail
½ C. brown sugar
1 C. chopped walnuts, toasted

For the topping
1 stick butter
3/4 C. sugar
½ C. evaporated milk
1 tsp. vanilla
1 C. flaked coconut

Directions

Combine the flour, sugar, cinnamon and baking soda in a bowl. Make a well in the center. Add eggs and fruit cocktail and stir gently. Pour into a buttered and floured 9x13 pan. Sprinkle brown sugar and nuts over the top. Bake at 350°F. for approximately forty-five minutes. Meanwhile, bring butter, sugar and milk for topping to a boil in a small pan over high heat. Boil for three minutes. Remove from heat and add the vanilla and coconut. Pour boiling hot over the cake as soon as it comes out of the oven.

Serves 12

French Vanilla Ice Cream

This was supposed to be the perfect ending to our *Titanic* dinner. I made it in an ice cream maker at home, ahead of time, packed it in an ice chest and brought it to be stored in the ship's freezer. Unfortunately, the *Jeremiah O'Brien's* freezers were all shut off for some reason so we had to use ice and the crew's refrigerator to keep the ice cream cold. By the time our guests were ready for dessert, we had French Vanilla pudding instead of ice cream. The best laid plans, etc. But it's a sumptuous dish. Just use your ice cream maker and serve it immediately.

Directions

In a heavy saucepan, warm the light cream and vanilla bean over medium heat until small bubbles just start to form around the edges of the pan. Remove from heat, cover and let stand for fifteen minutes.

Meanwhile, in a large bowl, whisk together egg yolks and sugar until pale and slightly thickened, about two minutes. Remove vanilla bean from pot. Gradually whisk warmed cream into egg mixture.

Return the mixture to the saucepan and cook over medium heat, stirring

Ingredients

2 C. light cream
1 vanilla bean, halved
  lengthwise
5 egg yolks
2/3 C. granulated sugar
1 C. whipping cream

NOTE:
Once again, it's worth the effort to use a real vanilla bean. The flavor is memorable.

Because the Jeremiah O'Brien *is a living museum ship commemorating the merchant marine in World War II, one finds frequent reminders of that era such as this poster in the gunner's mess and the poster in the crew mess, below. Photo: author.*

constantly, for five minutes or until thick enough to coat the back of a spoon.

Remove from heat and blend in whipping cream. Place, uncovered, in refrigerator and cool completely, stirring often.

Pour mixture into ice-cream maker and freeze according to manufacturer's instructions.

Serves 4-6.

Left, the crew mess set for lunch on "steaming weekend." One advantage of the coal-fired range is its ability to retain heat. Here, lunch is stacked atop pie tins to keep warm while the crew attends a meeting in #2 tween deck. Photos: author.

Joe Froggers

This is a traditional fisherman's cookie from Marblehead, Massachusetts. Legend says they were created by an African-American man known as Uncle Joe who had a reputation for making the best molasses cookies in town. They were called Joe Froggers because they were made by Uncle Joe and they were fat and dark like the frogs that lived in the pond near his house. The cookie was a favorite with fishermen because it stayed soft, no matter how long it was stored. Uncle Joe attributed the cookies' softness to rum and ocean salt water. Whatever the reason, they are delicious. They've always disappeared after a few days so I can't testify to the lasting softness.

Ingredients

7 C. flour
1 TBS. salt
1 TBS. ground ginger
1 tsp. ground cloves
1 tsp. grated nutmeg
½ tsp. ground allspice
3/4 C. water
1/4 C. rum (preferably, Myers dark)
2 tsp. baking soda
2 C. dark molasses
1 C. butter
2 C. sugar

Directions

Mix the flour and spices in a medium bowl and set aside. Combine the water and rum and stir with the baking soda into the molasses. Cream the shortening and sugar in a large bowl, add the dry ingredients and the rum mixture and blend. Refrigerate overnight.

Roll the cookie dough to ¼-inch thick on a floured board. Cut with a three-inch round cutter and place on a buttered cookie sheet. Bake for ten to twelve

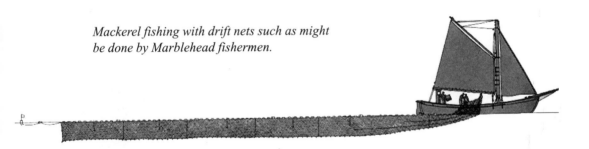

Mackerel fishing with drift nets such as might be done by Marblehead fishermen.

minutes in a preheated 375°F. oven. Let stand for a minute or two before removing to prevent breaking.

Makes about four dozen.

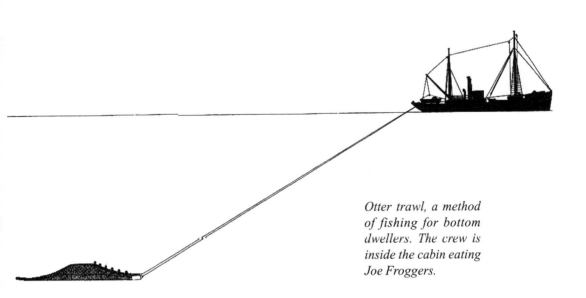

Otter trawl, a method of fishing for bottom dwellers. The crew is inside the cabin eating Joe Froggers.

Key Lime Pie

Chief Steward Jim Hallstrom making key lime pie for the volunteer crew. Photo: Author.

This is one of those recipes that takes on an almost religious significance in some people's minds. The purists say that a true Key Lime Pie can only be made with limes grown in the Florida Keys (where the recipe originates). Other proponents claim it must be thickened with condensed milk, not gelatin or corn starch; and it can't have a meringue or whipped cream topping; and, finally, it should be pale yellow, rather than green, in color. If you're willing to "settle" for local limes, I'm sure you'll find this recipe a winner, as did our guests at the *Matsonia* dinner we served on the *Jeremiah O'Brien*.

Directions

Beat the egg yolks until they are light and lemon colored. Add the milk, lime juice and the grated lime. Pour the custard into the pie shell and bake at 350°F. for about fifteen minutes or until it sets. Refrigerate before serving.

The pies going into the oven. Photo: Author.

Ingredients

1 baked pie shell
3 egg yolks
juice of six limes (½ C.)
2 tsp. grated lime rind
1-15 oz. can sweetened
  condensed milk

NOTES:
1. **The balance of the lime flavors can be delicate. It depends on how strongly flavored your limes are. Adjust the quantity of juice to zest up or down accordingly.**
2. **An interesting variation is to use a graham cracker shell instead of the standard flour pie shell.**
3. **Try covering the pie with meringue to which you've added 1 tsp. of lime juice before baking. (I can hear all those purists complaining already).**
4. **And a couple of drops of green food coloring will give it a nice "lime" appearance (now they're rolling over in their graves).**

Rhubarb Cobbler

Ingredients

1 C. flour
3/4 C. oatmeal
1 tsp. ground cinnamon
1 C. brown sugar
1 stick (½ C.) butter,
  melted
1 C. sugar
1 C. water
3 TBS. corn starch
1 tsp. vanilla extract
4 C. sliced rhubarb

This is another recipe that Rich Vannucci talked the Navy volunteer cooks out of. He says it is "great." And I know the only complaint among the *O'Brien*'s crew is that it isn't served often enough.

Directions

Combine flour, oatmeal, cinnamon, brown sugar and butter. Press half of the mixture into an 8x8 pan. Combine sugar, water, cornstarch and vanilla in a medium saucepan and cook over medium heat until very thick. Add rhubarb and mix thoroughly. Spread into pan and top with remaining oatmeal mixture. Bake in a preheated 350°F. oven for one hour.

Serves 10-12

Rich Vannucci serving crew lunch during a steaming weekend — the one weekend (3rd) of the month when the engine is run while the ship is alongside the dock so the public can view its operation. Photo: author.

Mocha Cake

This recipe is based on a cake called Mocha Marjolaine, a traditional dessert found in Paris. It's complicated but fun. Just the ticket to satisfy your guests and family at Thanksgiving or Christmas when a little extra work is part of the holiday enjoyment. We served it as part of a dinner based on a menu from the Matson liner, *Matsonia*.

Directions

Preheat oven to 325°F. Line a 18x12x1 jelly roll pan with parchment. Blend hazelnuts, almonds, ½ C. sugar and flour in a processor until the nuts are finely ground. With an electric mixer, beat the egg whites and cream of tartar in a large bowl until soft peaks form. Gradually add the remaining ¼ C. of sugar, beating until stiff. Fold in the nut mixture in two additions and spread evenly in the prepared pan. Bake until the meringue is golden brown and dry to the touch, about twenty minutes. Cool in the pan on a rack.

Cut around the pan sides. With the help of the parchment, lift the meringue onto a work surface. Press a large sheet of waxed paper on the meringue to cover it. Using a scissors, cut through the

Ingredients

Nut Meringue
3/4 C. hazelnuts, toasted, husked
3/4 C. whole almonds, toasted
3/4 C. sugar
1½ TBS. all purpose flour
6 large egg whites
½ tsp. cream of tartar

Frosting
1¼ C. plus 2 TBS. whipping cream
16 oz. bittersweet or semisweet chocolate, finely chopped

Coffee Cream Filling
2/3 C. chilled whipping cream
2 tsp. instant espresso powder
2 tsp. sugar

toasted hazelnuts

NOTES:
1. **A paper grocery bag, cut to the right size, will do for parchment paper.**
2. **Be sure the nuts are toasted. The difference in flavor between toasted and untoasted nuts is astonishing.**

Author making the frosting for Mocha Cake. Photo: S. Rose.

parchment and waxed paper to create a 16-inch by 8-inch rectangle of meringue. Cut in half crosswise, then lengthwise, forming four 8-inch by 4-inch rectangles.

Prepare the frosting. Bring 1¼ C. cream to simmer in a heavy medium saucepan. Remove it from the heat. Add the chocolate and whisk until the mixture is smooth. Transfer ¼ C. of the frosting to a small bowl, add the remaining 2 TBS. of cream to this to make a light frosting. Refrigerate the light frosting until cold, at least thirty minutes. Also refrigerate the dark frosting until it is cold, stirring frequently, for about one hour.

Prepare the coffee cream. Beat the chilled whipping cream, instant espresso powder and sugar in a medium bowl until stiff peaks form. Refrigerate.

Place a cake rack on a work surface. Peel the waxed paper and parchment off one rectangle and place it on the rack. Spread this layer with 1/3 C. of the dark frosting. Remove papers from second rectangle of cake and place it on top of the dark-frosted first layer. Whisk the light frosting until it is thick and spread it over the second layer. Peel the papers off the

The Matsonia *on a rare visit to Seattle. Photo: Joe Williamson.*

third layer and place it on top of the second. Spread this layer with half of the coffee cream. Cover and refrigerate the remaining coffee cream. Remove the papers from the fourth rectangle of cake and place it on top of the coffee cream-covered third layer. Spread ½ C. dark frosting in a thin layer over the top and sides to form a smooth surface. Refrigerate on rack for forty-five minutes.

Place the cake on its rack on a large sheet of aluminum foil. Stir the remaining dark frosting over very low heat until it is just warm enough to pour. Pour the dark frosting over the cake and, working quickly with an icing spatula, smooth the top and sides for an even coverage. Refrigerate until firm, at least 2 hours.

With a metal spatula, transfer the cake to a serving platter. Rewhip the remaining coffee cream and pipe it in a decorative pattern on top of the torte. Garnish with whole toasted hazelnuts and serve.

Serves 10.

Ricotta Zeppole

Ingredients

1 C. flour
1 tsp. baking powder
2 TBS. sugar
1 TBS. vanilla
2 eggs
1 lb. ricotta cheese
Olive oil for deep frying
Powdered sugar

NOTE:
Pine nuts and/or lemon peel can be added to the mix for a variation.

Rich Vannucci is part of the galley crew on the *O'Brien* that cooks for the ship's crew. His Italian heritage comes into play in many of the dishes he makes. This one gets snapped up as soon as it's cool enough to handle. Its roots are in the Calabria region of southern Italy.

Directions

Heat oil to proper temperature for deep frying (375°F.). Mix all the ingredients together. Form into walnut sized balls. Fry in small batches. When cool, sprinkle with powdered sugar.

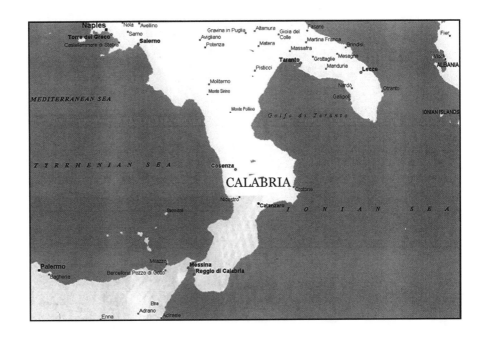

Shrewsbury Cakes

Although called cakes, they are really a cookie or, in the British vernacular, a biscuit. This is another recipe we used in our "Patrick O'Brian Dinner." It is simple, tasty and always brings out requests for more.

Directions

Cream the butter and sugar together until fluffy. Add the egg, brandy, coriander and mace. Mix well. Sift the flour (and salt, if appropriate) into the butter mixture, and work in thoroughly. Shape the dough into a ball, wrap it in plastic wrap and chill until firm, about one hour.

Preheat oven to 350°F. Working with half the dough at a time, roll out dough on a floured board to about ¼ inch thickness. Cut into squares or diamonds with a knife, or into shapes with a cookie cutter. Combine the scraps and roll them out again and recut as often as necessary. If the dough becomes sticky add more flour.

Place fairly close together on lightly greased cookie sheets. Bake nine to ten minutes. Let cool slightly before transferring to racks.

Makes about 4 dozen cookies.

Ingredients

½ lb. (2 sticks) butter
3/4 C. sugar
1 egg
2 TBS. brandy
4 tsp. freshly ground coriander
½ tsp. mace
3 C. flour
½ tsp. salt (if using unsalted butter)

NOTE:
Beware of rolling these too thin or baking them too long. Their distinctive flavor depends on not letting them brown. They should be barely golden around the edges.

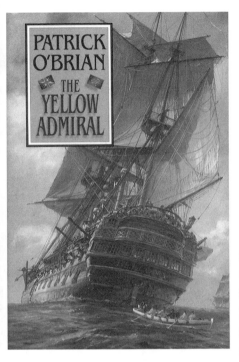

These work especially well in the *O'Brien*'s coal-fired stove, possibly because of the type of heat involved. We covered them with foil while baking, then removed the foil and put them back in for one minute, to brown them slightly. The cookies are light, taste pleasantly unusual and, although excellent when cooled, are best while still warm.

(I've never used a cookie recipe out of any cookbook that produced the quantity of cookies it claims, unless, of course, you make tiny cookies for people with tiny appetites. The original recipe said it made 6-8 dozen. Hah! This recipe tells it like it is.)

Spotted Dog with Custard Sauce

The British have a tradition of boiled puddings like no other country. Plum duff, Christmas pudding, spotted dog, spotted dick and boiled baby are a few that come to mind. That some of these are so oddly named is because they came from a time, centuries ago, when such names were considered pleasantly descriptive. (I guess you had to be there.) Nonetheless, a good boiled pudding is a delight. We served this as one of our desserts for the HMS *Surprise* raffle prize dinner in which we recreated a menu from the Patrick O'Brian stories on the *Jeremiah O'Brien*. Jack Aubrey probably would have enjoyed that coincidence of names.

Ingredients

For the pudding
4 C. flour
¼ C. sugar
½ tsp. salt
1½ tsp. cinnamon
¼ tsp. nutmeg
1 3/4 C. currants
½ lb. suet, grated fine
1 C. milk
2 eggs, lightly beaten

For the custard sauce
4 egg yolks
¼ C. sugar
pinch of salt
1¼ C. milk
¼ C. heavy cream
4 drops rose water
1½ TBS. brandy

Directions

In a large bowl, mix the flour, sugar, salt, cinnamon and nutmeg. Stir in the currants. Mix in the suet. Add the milk and eggs and work the mixture with your hands. Scrape the batter into a greased six-cup pudding mold. Place in a pot of boiling water, cover and steam for 2 hours.

Meanwhile, make the custard sauce. In the top of a double boiler, beat the

NOTE:
If you don't have a pudding mold, wrap the dough in cheesecloth or a clean dish towel, tie up the top, place in a colander and put the colander in the boiling water. Because the idea is to steam the pudding rather than boil it, the colander legs should be high enough to keep the pudding above the water level.

Chief Steward Jim Hallstrom, right, and Joe Guzzetta discuss upcoming events while preparing dessert for a volunteer crew lunch. Photo: Author.

yolks with the sugar and add the salt. Add the milk and cream and stir. Set the pot over gently boiling water and cook, stirring constantly, until the custard is thick enough to coat the back of a spoon (about ten minutes). Remove from heat and stir in the rose water and brandy. Pour over individual servings of pudding.

Serves 8.

The normal reaction when first hearing the name of this dish might be, yuch! But you really should try it. The pudding tastes wonderful and it's a delightful finish to a good dinner.

Steaming the pudding requires frequent stoking to keep the temperature even. Photo: Author.

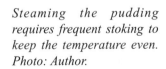

Zabaglione with Champagne and Raspberries

The SS Mariposa *is greeted on her maiden voyage in October 1956 by the pilot schooner* California. *Photo: Matson Lines.*

This is a delicious cold variation on the classic Italian dessert which is usually served warm. The champagne gives it an extra little touch that elevates it above the ordinary. We served this as one of the desserts for an Italian night dinner based on a menu from the SS *Mariposa* on one of her voyages in the late 1950s. Everyone loved it.

Ingredients

5 large egg yolks
½ C. sugar
½ C. champagne
2/3 C. well chilled
    whipping cream
1 pint fresh raspberries
mint leaves

Directions

In a metal bowl, beat the yolks and sugar together with an electric mixer for about three minutes or until the mixture is thick and pale. Beat in the champagne. Set the bowl over a saucepan of simmering water and beat the mixture with a hand-held mixer for three to five minutes or until it is about four times its original volume and just hot to the touch. Transfer the bowl to a larger bowl of ice and cold water and whisk the mixture until it is cold. Beat the cream in a chilled bowl with an electric mixer until it holds soft peaks. Fold 1/3 of it into the yolk mixture, then, gently but thoroughly, fold in the remaining whipped cream. Divide the raspberries between eight wineglasses, spoon the zabaglione over them and garnish with mint leaves.

Serves 8.

This is one of a series of menu covers that American President Lines did for their fleet during the 1960s. It captures the essence of the captain's responsibilities. Courtesy George Bonawit.

Breakfast

S.S. AMERICA

FRUITS - FRUCHT
Fresh Frozen Raspberries with Cream   Sliced Fresh Pineapple
Sliced Frozen Peaches with Syrup   Frozen Blueberries with Cream
Iced Melon Balls   Sliced Banana with Cream
Iced Grapefruit   Apple   Orange
Juices: Sauerkraut, Orange or Sweet Apple
Stewed Fruits: Prunes, Pears or Mixed

CEREALS - FRUHSTÜCK CEREALS
H-O Oats   Boiled Hominy Grits
Corn Soya Shreds   Sugar Pops   Pep   Wheaties   Raisin Bran
Triscuits   Shredded Wheat   Pablum   Corn Flakes
Grapenuts   Frosted Flakes   Puffed Rice   Krumbles
All Bran   Post Toasties   Puffed Wheat
40% Bran Flakes   Rice Krispies   Grapenut Flakes

FISH - FISCH
Broiled English Kippered Herring   Finnan Haddie in Double Cream

EGGS - EIER
Boiled   Poached   Shirred   Buttered   Fried with Ham or Bacon
Scrambled: (Rühreier) with Smoked Salmon, Swiss Cheese or Plain
Omelettes: (Eierkuchen) with Mushrooms, Sardines, Chicken Livers or Plain

MEAT - FLEISCH-GERICHT
Baked Corned Beef Hash, Demi Glace

FROM THE GRILL - VOM ROST
Chopped Tenderloin Steak (Gehacktes Beef Steak)
American Bacon   Yorkshire Ham   Country Sausages
Amerikanischer Frühstück Speck   Yorkshire Schinken   Bauernwürstchen

POTATOES - KARTOFFELN
Boiled, Mashed or Lyonnaise (Gekochter, Puree oder Bratkartoffeln)

COLD DISHES - KALTER AUFSCHNITT
Assorted Delicatess Plate, Garni
(Gemischter Kalter Aufschnitt, Garniert)
Various Kinds of Fresh and Smoked Sausages
(Verschiedene Frische und Geräucherte Wurst)

Wheat or Buckwheat Griddle Cakes with Maple Syrup
(Weizen oder Buchweizen Pfannkuchen)
Vienna Rolls   Melba, Milk, Buttered or Dry Toast   Zwieback
Assorted Sweet Buns   Ry-Krisp   Tea Biscuits

PRESERVES
Assorted Jams (Gelee)   Orange Marmalade   Strained Honey (Honig)

BEVERAGES
Coffee   Cocoa   Chocolate   Fresh Milk
Kaffee   Kakao   Schokolade   Frische Milch
Sanka Coffee   Postum   Teas: English Breakfast, Ceylon or Orange Pekoe

WB-CCBG-4   Sunday, August 14, 1955

UNITED STATES LINES

S.S. PRESIDENT TRUMAN
THURSDAY MAY 11, 1978   VOYAGE 67   OAKLAND, CAL
CAPTAIN W.Q. SEDDON   COMMANDING

BREAKFAST

CHILLED ASSORTED FRUIT JUICES   FRESH GRAPEFRUIT HALF   FIGS
HOT ROLLED OATS CEREAL   ASSORTED DRY CEREALS
GRILLED SMOKED BREAKFAST HAM   CREAMED CHIP BEEF ON TOAST POINT
EGGS TO ORDER   WESTERN OMELET   BACON OMELET   PLAIN OMELET
PLAIN OR RAISIN FRENCH TOAST   WAFFLES   HASH BROWNS   RICE
COFFEE   TEA   MILK   COCOA   CHOCOLATE   OVALTINE   SANKA
ASSORTED JAMS AND JELLIES   MAPLE SYRUP   HONEY   MARMALADE

BREAKFAST

S. S. MARIPOSA

MONDAY, JANUARY 9, 1978

...yrup   Stewed Prunes in Syrup   Sliced California Orange
Cold Half Grapefruit, Maraschino   Chilled Papaya   Baked Apple   Frosted Elberta Peaches
Iced Guava Nectar, Orange, Prune, Pineapple or Tomato Juice

CEREALS
Rolled Oats   Cracked Wheat   Corn Flakes   Special K   Puffed Wheat   Shredded Wheat   Pep

...red Boiled Potatoes

Poached Eggs on Toast   Boiled Eggs
...sh Sauce, Smoked Salmon or Plain
...Stewed Tomatoes, Ham or Plain
, Canadian Bacon or Plain

Broiled Center Cut Ham   Grilled Breakfast or Canadian Bacon
Top Sirloin of Beef Patty)
...st en Casserole

COLD BUFFET
Cold Roast Beef   Roast Spring Lamb, Mint Jelly   Assorted Smoked Sliced California Sausage
Imported Italian Salami and Swiss Cheese

SWEET ROLLS, WAFFLES, TOAST
Assorted Sweet Rolls   Muffin of the Day   Danish Coffee Cake
Blueberries, Buckwheat or Plain Griddle Cakes, Waffles
Served with Honey, Whipped or Melted Butter, Maple or Boysenberry Syrup
Whole Wheat, White, Raisin, Buttered, Cinnamon, Dry, Melba or French Toast

JAMS, JELLIES
Orange Marmalade   Guava Jelly   Strawberry Preserve   Blackberry or Papaya-Pineapple Jam

---

SS PACIFIC VICTORY
SATURDAY JUNE 14 1969
BREAKFAST
ORANGE JUICE   HOT CAKES OR FRENCH TOAST
MANGOES   ASST DRY CEREALS
FARINA   FRIED POTATOES

EGGS TO ORDER
GREEN ONION OMELET
GRILLED BACON OR SAUSAGE LINKS
COFFEE   TEA   COCOA   FRESH MILK

Breakfasts

ost nutritionists consider breakfast the most important meal of the day. It's been ten or twelve hours since your last meal (you're "breaking" a "fast" of that long) so you should make it a good one. You'll have another meal in four or five hours and another four or five hours after that — lunch and dinner should be lighter to sustain the energy you develop by having a good breakfast.

Our raffle prize dinners are evening meals, but the regular galley crew cooks breakfast on steaming weekends and before each of the annual cruises in May and October. At home, breakfast is a favorite meal on weekends and holidays, when there's time to cook without the pressure of getting to work on time.

Here are a few favorites from Sunday mornings, old steamship and windjammer days and the era of the great passenger liners.

Breakfast Crêpes

Sightseeing boats on the Seine in Paris.

In Paris one finds crêpe stands on the streets like hot dog stands in America. The crêpes are made while you wait, then covered with melted butter or powdered sugar, or a fruit or nut paste according to your desires. They offer at least a dozen flavors to choose from. Our favorite was chestnut. In any case, they are served fresh and hot. You can duplicate the experience at home with this recipe.

Ingredients

1 1/8 C. flour
1 TBS. sugar
salt
3 eggs
1½ C. milk
1 TBS. melted butter
1 TBS. brandy
powdered sugar

Directions

Beat the eggs and combine with the flour, sugar, a pinch of salt and the milk until a smooth batter is formed. Stir in the butter and brandy. Let sit for two hours.

Heat a crêpe pan (an omelet pan or frying pan will work) over medium heat until hot. Melt a teaspoon of butter on the pan, remove from stove and pour about one tablespoon of batter on the pan, quickly turning it to make about a five-inch circle. When set, turn once and cook the other side.

To serve, place a tablespoon of filling in a line along the center of the crêpe and roll into a tube shape around it. Sprinkle with powdered sugar.

Serves 6.

NOTES:
1. Crêpes can be kept warm in a low (200°F.) oven until ready to serve.
2. Use anything you like for the filling: orange or lemon marmalade, raspberry jam, fresh sliced fruit, blueberries, etc.
3. For an interesting variation, sprinkle with vanilla powder instead of powdered sugar.

Buckwheat Cakes

Ingredients

½ C. white flour
1½ C. buckwheat flour
1 tsp. baking soda
½ tsp. double-acting
  baking powder
½ tsp. salt
3¼ C. buttermilk
2 TBS. melted butter

Buckwheat has a distinctive flavor that makes a pleasant change from the traditional white flour pancake. It's used a lot more in European cooking, especially Russian, than American. Buckwheat flour is actually ground from the small, seedlike fruit of the buckwheat, an Asian plant that produces clusters of small, white or pink flowers. The flavor is quite different from wheat flour. Buckwheat cakes were a favorite on the SS *America* on her trans-Atlantic runs.

Directions

Mix all the ingredients together and beat until just blended. Pour enough batter from a ladle onto a buttered griddle at medium heat to make four-inch cakes. When bubbles form, turn the cake and brown the other side. Turn only once.

Serves 4.

The SS America *as she appeared around 1950. U.S. Maritime Commission.*

Burgoo

The typical dress of "Jack Tar," the lower deck sailor of Admiral Nelson's day (early 1800s).

This is an old seafaring dish that dates back to the early days of the British Navy. It could be easily prepared, regardless of the weather, giving Jack Tar a nourishing meal even in a howling gale. Unfortunately for the British sailor, its ease of preparation made it a popular dish with lazy cooks and it was often served in any weather, and sometimes more than once a day. It's included in the interest of preserving the old seaman's dishes.

Directions

Stir the oats into the water in a medium-sized pan. Set over medium heat and bring to a boil. Reduce the heat and simmer for fifteen minutes, stirring constantly. Remove from heat, add salt, butter and sugar, stirring until dissolved.

Serves 4.

Ingredients

2 C. steel-cut oats
4 C. water
1 tsp. salt
3 TBS. butter
4 tsp. sugar

NOTE:
This becomes a much more palatable dish with the addition of some milk or cream, substituting dark brown sugar for regular white, and adding raisins, a chopped fresh peach or other fruit.

Cottage Cheese Pancakes

Ingredients

4 eggs separated
1 C. sour cream
1 C. small curd cottage
   cheese
1 C. white flour
1 tsp. baking soda
2 TBS. sugar
2 TBS. vegetable oil

Here is an interesting recipe for flapjacks when you want something with a slightly different flavor. At first glance it might sound heavy but they come out as light and tasty as any pancake and they have a unique and enjoyable flavor. The steamer *Queen* featured flannel cakes, which may have been similar to these, on her menu in 1917.

Directions

Beat the egg whites to the stiff peak stage. In a separate bowl, beat the yolks slightly, add in the other ingredients and mix well. Gently fold in the egg whites. Heat the griddle or a skillet over medium heat. Add small amount of vegetable oil. When oil is hot ladle ¼ C. of the batter for each pancake onto the surface, turning once when the bottom is browned.

Serves 4.

PACIFIC STEAMSHIP COMPANY

ON BOARD S. S. QUEEN   M. F. TARPEY, Commander

FRIDAY Nov. 2 1917

BREAKFAST

California Oranges   Grape Fruit   Iced Casaba Melon
Prunes with   Cranberry Sauce   Stewed White Figs
Preserved Plums   Stewed
Orange Marmalade   Assorted Jams

(CREAM SERVED WITH ALL CEREALS)

Rolled Oats   Egg-O-See   Shredded Wheat   Grape Nuts
Boiled Rice   Post Toasties   Corn Flakes

Flounder Lemon Butter
Broiled Sirloin Steak and Onions
Grilled Mutton Chops Saratoga Chips
Corned Beef Hash with Poached Egg
Club House Sausage with Rice
Fried Sugar Cured Ham
Grilled Breakfast Bacon
Fried   Boiled   Scrambled Poached or Shirred
Omelet a la Queen   Plain Omelet
Fried Potatoes   Boiled Irish Potatoes

Hot Rolls   Dry or Buttered Toast
Soda Biscuits
Flannel Cakes with Log Cabin Syrup or Honey

Tea   Coffee   English Breakfast Tea
Chocolate   Cocoa   Fresh Milk

Right, the SS Queen *loading passengers for the Seattle-San Francisco run around 1917. Photo Joe Williamson.*

Eggs and Chorizo

The SS *Jeremiah O'Brien* is based in San Francisco, a culinary crossroads. The city's restaurants are world famous with every type of cuisine represented — the standard international cuisines (Italian, French, Thai, etc.) to Greek, Ethiopian, Samoan to — well, you name it.

Less obvious, but equally flavorful is the cooking from immigrants that settled the area and adapted the native cooking of their homeland to the produce, fish and meats of the local area. North Beach and Fisherman's Wharf have long been popular for Italian cooking, California style. Down and up the coast and inland, one finds Portuguese-California cooking, Basque-California, Mexican-California and so on.

One influence that is often overlooked is that of the pre-Gold Rush settlers: the Swiss, the Russians and especially the Californios — those of Mexican ancestry born in California during the Land Grant era. It is this last group that gives us Rancho California cooking, a unique and tasty cuisine that relies heavily on common ingredients of that era — chiles, corn, beef, pork, garlic. All of this prelude gets us to one of my favorite breakfasts, eggs and chorizo.

Mexican Chorizo is a spicy sausage, and it goes great with scrambled *huevos* (eggs), unlike the Spanish chorizo which is rather dry and tastes better in soups and stews. You start by making your own sausage.

Ingredients

2 lb. lean pork, cut in small pieces
10 oz. pork fat, chilled and cut in pieces
2 cloves minced garlic
3 tsp. oregano
½ tsp. freshly ground black pepper
2 tsp. cumin seeds
3 tsp. salt
1 TBS. sweet paprika
6 TBS. chile powder
¼ C. water
1/3 C. cider vinegar
2 TBS. port wine

NOTE:
The sausage can be frozen if not used immediately.

Directions

Mix all the spices together. Add the water to form a paste. In a food processor grind the pork and fat, about 1/3 at a time, adding a small amount of the spice paste to the mix. In a large bowl, add the remaining paste to the ground pork, mixing with your hands. Place in a refrigerator for twenty-four hours to let the flavors meld.

Fry the sausage, loose, over medium heat until done.

Scramble two eggs per person in a separate pan.

Serve together.

Serves up to 12.

The most prominent Californio in Northern California was General Mariano Vallejo. He managed a vast estate at Petaluma and his Petaluma adobe was a center of commerce (and cooking) in the early days. The Vallejo Petaluma Adobe is now a state park and often stages "Living History Days." After the Gold Rush the docks at Petaluma, right, frequently saw coastal schooners and shallow draft boats alongside. Photo: San Francisco Maritime Historical Park.

French Toast

Traditionally, French toast is made with stale bread. In the San Francisco area, however, we have sourdough bread, which doesn't need to be stale to make good French toast. If you can't find sourdough in your area, use French bread that's been sitting around for a few days. French toast was a favorite on the *President Truman* in the late 1970s.

Directions

In a large bowl combine the milk, eggs, sugar and vanilla and mix thoroughly. Soak the slices of bread in this mixture for a few minutes, turning once or twice to ensure complete saturation.

Meanwhile, melt the butter in a heavy skillet and add the vegetable oil. When this mixture is quite hot, fry the soaked bread slices until golden brown. Sprinkle with the cinnamon/sugar mixture just before serving. Serve with syrup.

Serves 4.

Ingredients

1 C. milk
2 large eggs, well beaten
¼ C. sugar
1 TBS. vanilla extract
4 slices sourdough bread, cut about 1½ inches thick
2 TBS. butter
2 TBS. vegetable oil
1 tsp. cinnamon mixed with 2 tsp. powdered sugar

NOTES:
1. For an added dimension, include ¼ C. Myers dark rum.
2. For a tasty variation, instead of syrup, top the French toast with sliced white peaches and fresh blueberries.

Kedgeree

Ingredients

1 lb. poached finnan
   haddie (smoked
   haddock) in small
   pieces
2 C. cold, cooked rice
3 TBS. butter
5 hard-boiled eggs,
   coarsely chopped
3 TBS. whipping cream
½ tsp. dry mustard
   mixed with ½ tsp.
   water
salt
pepper
cayenne
lemon juice

This is a delightful dish and a pleasant change from the normal breakfast fare. It comes from India, by way of England with a hint of Scotland thrown in. The original dish was known as *khichri* and was more of a lentil-based curry than anything else. By the time it passed through Great Britain many of the spices were deleted in favor of smoked fish. It makes a great breakfast dish, although it can be served at any time of day.

Directions

Melt the butter in a saucepan, add the fish and the rice and cook over medium heat, stirring occasionally, for five minutes. Reduce the heat, stir in the eggs, cream, mustard and other seasonings to taste and cook until heated through.

Serves 6

Kippered Herring

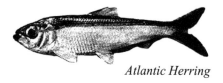

Atlantic Herring

This is a favorite breakfast on English ships and in many English and Scottish households — and in ours. In the U.S. it might be an acquired taste; not that many people have smoked fish for breakfast. But if you try kippers you won't soon forget them and will probably enjoy the dish again. Kippers were offered on the *America* in the mid-1950s.

Directions

This recipe works best if you give the potatoes a head start. Melt butter in frying pan over medium heat. Add oil and potatoes. Fry potatoes, uncovered for fifteen minutes, turning occasionally. Meanwhile, in a separate pan, fry mushrooms in some butter until the liquid has evaporated. Add onions and stir fry, turning frequently, until both are slightly brown. Combine potatoes and onion/mushroom mixture. Place frozen kippers, skin side up, on top of mixture, cover and cook for about ten minutes. Turn fish so skin side is down and cook, covered, for an additional ten minutes. Place fish on one side of plate, potatoes, onions and mushrooms on the other side.

The entire meal will be permeated with that great kipper flavor. Enjoy!

Serves 2.

Ingredients

1 pkg. frozen Scottish or Canadian kippers (2 fish per package)
4 medium russet potatoes, diced
1 medium onion, sliced thinly
¼ lb. mushrooms, sliced medium
1 TBS. butter
1 TBS. olive oil

Orange Pecan Waffles

Ingredients

½ C. toasted pecan
  pieces
1 1/3 C. white flour
2 TBS. sugar
4 tsp. baking powder
½ tsp. salt
grated rind of one
  orange
2 large eggs
¼ C. melted butter
1½ C. club soda

Waffles are crowd-pleasers and were standard fare on most freighters as well as on passenger liners. Light, crunchy, slightly sweet and warm, they can be covered with almost any topping you wish. The popularity of the Belgian waffles at the New York World's Fair of 1965 began the craze that is still going on. They were topped with whipped cream and fresh strawberries and the places that sold them always had the longest lines in the fair. This recipe is unusual, not for what goes on top but for what's inside. All you need for the top is a little melted butter and a sprinkle of powdered sugar or a dash of maple syrup.

Directions

Mix the pecans, flour, sugar, baking powder and salt in a blender until the pecans are finely ground. Pour mix into a large bowl, add orange peel and mix. Beat in eggs and butter. Add club soda, mixing completely. Cook immediately in preheated waffle iron. Serves 4

Even workaday freighters such as the Wesleyan Victory *featured waffles as part of their menu. Photo: U.S. Maritime Administration.*

Sky Blue

This is another seafaring dish that dates back at least 150 years. I don't know the derivation of the name, but your imagination could probably come up with something as good. Basically, we're talking about a form of gruel, but, once again, remember that to seafaring men on wind ships, anything was a pleasant change from their normal salt beef and weevil-laden hard tack.

Ingredients

½ C. pearl barley
1 cup seawater
butter
sugar
milk or cream

Directions

Place the water in a saucepan. Bring to a boil over high heat. Add barley, reduce heat to medium-low and boil for two hours. Stir occasionally and add more seawater if necessary. (You can substitute salt water for seawater.) Serve with butter, sugar and milk or cream to taste.

Serves 2.

The crew of the Monongahela *was probably familiar with "Sky Blue." Photo: Harry A. Kirwin.*

Steam Schooners

Ingredients

Pancakes
2 C. flour
2 TBS. sugar
4 tsp. baking powder
½ tsp. salt
2 eggs
1 3/4 C. milk
2 TBS. melted butter

Eggs
4 eggs
2 tsp. butter

Sausage
8 link pork sausages or
4 sausage patties

The steam schooner Admiral Nicholson *sailed for Admiral Line. Photo: Joe Williamson.*

Here's that dish mentioned in the introduction, named from the steam schooners that ran up and down the West Coast until World War II. Picture yourself on one of those coasters, tied alongside a pier somewhere in Oregon. The dark of night turns to a thick grey fog. The air is cool and crisp. As you put on your work clothes, you smell breakfast cooking in the galley. Soon, you are seated at the mess table with your shipmates; a mug of coffee steams in front of you as the messman brings out armloads of plates covered with pancakes topped with fried eggs and sausage.

Directions

Mix the flour, sugar, baking powder and salt. Beat two eggs, add them and the milk and melted butter to the dry ingredients, stirring gently. Pour enough batter to make an 8-inch pancake onto a lightly greased hot griddle over medium heat. When bubbles appear on the top, flip the cake and bake the other side.

Meanwhile, fry the eggs sunny side up, cook the sausage.

To serve, stack three pancakes on a plate, top with two eggs and place sausages on side. Serve with butter and maple syrup.

Serves 2.

The nucleus of the "raffle prize dinner crew." When all is said and done, it's not worth it unless you're having fun. Obviously, they enjoy it all. Left to right, Wes Masterson, author, Bev Masterson.

Recipe Index

General Index

Bibliography

Recipe Index

General Index

(page numbers in bold type indicate recipes)

c

BIBLIOGRAPHY

Archbold, Rick and Daba McCauley. *Last Dinner on the Titanic*. The Madison Press Limited: Toronto, 1997.

Beard, James. *Beard on Bread*. Alfred A. Knopf: New York, 1974.

Booth, Letha. *Williamsburg Cookbook, The*. The Colonial Williamsburg Foundation: Williamsburg, Virginia, 1976.

Cordingly, David, consulting Editor. *Pirates, Terror on the High Seas From the Caribbean to the South China Sea*. Turner Publishing, Inc.: Atlanta, 1996.

Goldsmith-Carter, George, *Sailors Sailors*, Paul Hamlyn: London, 1966.

Grossman, Anne Chotzinoff and Lisa Grossman Thomas. *Lobscouse & Spotted Dog*. W.W. Norton & Company: New York, London, 1997.

Jackson, June. *The Showboat Cookbook*. Wings Books: New York, 1996.

McMahan, Jacqueline Higuera. *California Rancho Cooking*. The Olive Press: Lake Hughes, CA, 1984.

Oliver, Sandra Louise. *Saltwater Foodways*. Mystic Seaport Museum: Mystic, Connecticut. 1995.

Rogozinski, Jan. *Pirates! Brigands, Buccaneers and Privateers in Fact, Fiction and Legend*. Facts on File, Inc: New York, 1995.

Warren, Janet. *Feast of Scotland, A*. Hodder and Stoughton Ltd.: London, 1979

Additional Recipes

Appetizers:

Recipe: _____
Ingredients

_____   _____

_____   _____

_____   _____

_____   _____

Directions

_____

_____

_____

_____

_____

Recipe: _____
Ingredients

_____   _____

_____   _____

_____   _____

Directions

_____

_____

_____

_____

Additional Recipes

Soups:

Recipe: _____
Ingredients

_____   _____

_____   _____

_____   _____

_____   _____

Directions

_____

_____

_____

_____

_____

Recipe: _____
Ingredients

_____   _____

_____   _____

_____   _____

Directions

_____

_____

_____

_____

Additional Recipes

Salads:

Recipe: _____

Ingredients

_____ _____

_____ _____

_____ _____

_____ _____

Directions

_____

_____

_____

_____

_____

Recipe: _____

Ingredients

_____ _____

_____ _____

_____ _____

Directions

_____

_____

_____

_____

Additional Recipes

Seafood:

Recipe: _____
Ingredients

_____   _____

_____   _____

_____   _____

_____   _____

Directions

_____

_____

_____

_____

_____

Recipe: _____
Ingredients

_____   _____

_____   _____

_____   _____

Directions

_____

_____

_____

_____

Additional Recipes

Main Courses:

Recipe: _____
Ingredients

_____   _____

_____   _____

_____   _____

_____   _____

Directions

_____

_____

_____

_____

_____

Recipe: _____
Ingredients

_____   _____

_____   _____

_____   _____

Directions

_____

_____

_____

_____

Additional Recipes

Main Courses:

Recipe: _____

Ingredients

_____   _____

_____   _____

_____   _____

_____   _____

Directions

_____

_____

_____

_____

Recipe: _____

Ingredients

_____   _____

_____   _____

_____   _____

Directions

_____

_____

_____

_____

Additional Recipes

Vegetables & Side Dishes:

Recipe: _____
Ingredients

_____   _____

_____   _____

_____   _____

_____   _____

Directions

_____

_____

_____

_____

Recipe: _____
Ingredients

_____   _____

_____   _____

_____   _____

Directions

_____

_____

_____

_____

Additional Recipes

Breads, Rolls & Biscuits:

Recipe: _____

Ingredients

_____   _____

_____   _____

_____   _____

_____   _____

Directions

_____

_____

_____

_____

Recipe: _____

Ingredients

_____   _____

_____   _____

_____   _____

Directions

_____

_____

_____

_____

Additional Recipes

Desserts:

Recipe: _____
Ingredients

_____   _____

_____   _____

_____   _____

_____   _____

Directions

_____

_____

_____

_____

Recipe: _____
Ingredients

_____   _____

_____   _____

_____   _____

Directions

_____

_____

_____

_____

Additional Recipes

Desserts:

Recipe: _____

Ingredients

_____   _____

_____   _____

_____   _____

_____   _____

Directions

_____

_____

_____

_____

Recipe: _____

Ingredients

_____   _____

_____   _____

_____   _____

Directions

_____

_____

_____

_____